Rogha Dánta

Death in the Land of Youth

Do Bheití

Rogha Dánta
Death in the Land of Youth

Seán Ó Tuama

Translations / Versions by
Peter Denman and Seán Ó Tuama

Introduction by Robert Welch

CORK UNIVERSITY PRESS

First published in 1997 by
Cork University Press
University College
Cork
Ireland

British Library Cataloguing in Publication Data
A CIP catalogue record for this book is available from the British Library.

ISBN 1 85918 157 0 hardback
1 85918 158 9 paperback

Typeset by Tower Books of Ballincollig, Co. Cork
Printed by ColourBooks, Baldoyle, Co. Dublin

Contents

Introduction vii
Chronology xxi

I *Fuinneoga/Windows*

Fuinneoga '94/Windows '94 2
Ise Seachtó hOcht, Eisean Ochtó Ceathair/She Being Seventy-Eight, He Being Eighty-Four 4
An File dá Bhean/The Poet to his Wife 6
Cá Siúlfam/Where Shall We Walk 8
Siúlóid in Éirinn/A Walk in Ireland 10
Rousseau na Gaeltachta/A Gaeltacht Rousseau 12
Christy Ring/Christy Ring 14
An Cat/The Cat 18
Maymount: Tigh Victeoireach a Leagadh/Maymount: a Victorian House, Demolished 20
Bás Fómhair/Elegy on the Death of a Young Married Woman 24
Abair do Phaidir/Say a Prayer 26
Cluiche / Love-Game 28
Rince Seite/Set Dance 30
Coinní Iarbháis/Assignations with the Dead 32
Ag na Soilse Dearga/At the Red Lights in Paris 34
Beannacht Abhaile/Greetings from Abroad 36
Asailín Pharis/The Little Paris Donkey 38
Amhrán Grá/The Musicians' Love Song 40
Trí Phictiúr dem Namhaid/Three Views of my Antagonist 42
Ar an dTraein go Dún Éideann/On the Express to Edinburgh 44
Ar Bhás Carad/Elegy on the Death of a Friend 48
Nuair Shínfead Siar/Before they Bundle up this House of Clay 50

II *Pictiúir Tí agus Tíre/Interiors and Exteriors*

Cág/The Crow 54
Uisce/Water 54

Díle Samhraidh / Summer Rain 56
Grian Fómhair / Autumn Sunlight 56
Bó Uaigneach / Cow 58
Ceol Fómhair / Autumn Music 58
Taibhreamh / A Dream 58
Leac Oighir sa Chiúnas / Ice Quietly 60
Sollúntacht an Mhion-Éin / The Solemnity of a Minor Bird 60
Múscailt Bhréige / A False Awakening 62

III *Aidhe! / Aye!*
(From a Greek Diary / Dréachtaí Dialainne, 1977-80)

Do Stoitheas Luibh / I Picked a Herb 66
Seilbh Tí, 1977 / Moving In, 1977 66
An t-Arán Laethúil / Daily Bread 68
Ella! / Ella! 70
Ar Ghrinneall Abhann / On the River Bed 70
Sagart Gréagach / The Greek Priest 72
Ceann Cait / Owl 72
Claisceadal na nAsal / Donkey Concert 74
Ógbhean Ghréagach / The Greek Girl 76
Múchadh na Gréine / The Sun Put Out 76
Seanbhean Ghréagach / Old Greek Woman 78
Turasóirí, 1980 / Tourists, 1980 78

IV *Turasóir sa Ghréig / A Tourist in Greece*

Síos Linn / Greek Waters 84
Siúlóid sa Chréit / A Walk in Crete 84
Ar Bhóthar Cnoic sa Chréit / A Mountain Road in Crete 86
Cumar ins an Chréit / A Ravine in Crete 86
Comharthaí Aimsire / Heat and Decay 88
'Besides, who knows before the end what light may shine' / 'Besides, who knows before the end what light may shine' 88
Anocht sa Ghréig Cuimhním mar Chímís chūgainn ar dTúis an Solas Tóirse / I Recall Tonight in Greece 92
Tigh sa Ghréig / A House in Greece 94

V *Baoithín a d'Fhill ar Éirinn (1956) (dréacht as) / Baoithín Returns to Ireland (1956) (an extract)* 99

Introduction

'. . . what most likely is eternal is Earth not Man.'

('Celebration and Mortality: A View of Irish Literature', unpublished lecture)

So concludes a lecture written for an international writers' symposium, and as a critical and evaluative statement it is entirely characteristic of Ó Tuama's style of thought, his method of critical analysis, and the pressure of his creative impulse. This arresting statement comes, in the context of the essay, out of a scrupulous, painstaking examination of the ways in which various writers in the Gaelic tradition perceive reality, celebrate existence, and respond to the natural world. He cites the report that Alexander the Great had concerning the Continental Celts – that they feared nothing except that the sky might fall; he comments on the pristine phenomenality of the early Irish nature lyric; he addresses the modern poet Nuala Ní Dhomhnaill's capacity to link 'fertile events' in nature to human sexuality and then, in this brilliant concluding move he strikes to the core of the subject he is seeking to penetrate. He argues that one of the elements that subsists at all phases of Irish tradition is a sense that the ever-changingness of being is what is truly permanent, and that Irish literary art is at its most commanding and authoritative when the personality of the writer accommodates itself to permanent preoccupations. Here we have such a personality.

Stated here is one of these apparent contradictions in life and art that Ó Tuama has spent years of patient toil, as teacher, artist, and critic unravelling: that art (whether poetry, or prose, or whatever) is really of little interest to us unless it speaks to us personally; and yet it cannot do that unless it also attains some degree of impersonality, of formal distance. As a teacher in the classroom he would worry at a problem like this tirelessly, patiently, so that his seminars on poetry became intellectual anatomies of the relation, the necessary relation, between emotion (personal emotion) and form (often traditional form). Any serious work of artistic creation, he would tell his students, resolves this apparent contradiction in new and surprising ways, but these will always be characterized by a human charge emanating from the personality of the author.

On the scales of Ó Tuama's critical and evaluative intelligence there is, on one side, the personal in all its fortuitousness amidst the riot of chance, of accident; on the other there are those 'ancient forms' (John Montague's phrase) which embrace much more than formal structure and involve the entire apparatus of perception and understanding of any given culture. Ó Tuama's conception of the formal structure of tradition derives ultimately from Corkery, his mentor, but, as he makes clear in an essay which is part homage to his old professor, part rebuke to deliberate misreadings of him, Corkery's view of cultural 'modes and forms' is much more extensive, coherent and omnivalent than is commonly thought. He quotes Corkery on the function of language in culture, comparing it to Claude Levi-Strauss's structuralist formulations:

> Amongst the modes and forms of a culture we may enumerate language . . . all the arts, social customs, games, etc. These . . . constitute a form of spiritual organism . . . Any part of them may at first view seem to be disparate genera: actually they harmonise one with another . . . *They are organically coordinated.*
>
> (*Repossessions*, 1995, p. 237)

As a critic and as a writer Ó Tuama seeks to set the balance trembling between the matrix (or matrices) of form — tradition, community, genre, convention, metric, place — and the individual, the personal. Once tension is registered, the writer's own personal being can find an impetus, an impulse, a rhythmic and immediate thrust which negotiates, and is fortified by, all those ambivalences and contradictions which in ordinary life remain disparate and unreconciled. Ó Tuama's critical and creative work are of a piece; he is like the scholar in the old Irish poem who compares his activity to that of his pet cat, Pangur Bán. Patient stillness and thinking and pondering are a preliminary to the sudden rush in which an experience or idea is completely apprehended — just as the cat pounds on its prey, after contained waiting. That is how the statement 'what most likely is eternal is Earth not Man' arrests us. In this bold stroke he identifies a permanent tendency in the Irish mentality and culture — a sense of conjoined mortality and celebration — and shows it operating with all the suddenness and immediacy of achieved poetry in Nuala Ní Dhomhnaill and in the Sweeney poet, the author of the twelfth-century *Buile Shuibhne*. Cultural tendency and individual expression are, in Corkery's phrase, 'organically coordinated'.

For a poet and artist who has, in a manner more familiar to, say, French or Latin-American cultural life than that of Ireland or England, combined a life of intellectual enquiry with artistic expression, it is not inappropriate to outline a couple of basic formal and aesthetic concerns, such as those accentuated above, before moving to some appraisal of a few key elements in Ó Tuama's poetry. A virtue he continually extols, in spite (or because of) his intellectual sophistication, is simplicity. And it is the direct and frank simplicity with which he approaches things that gives his verse its first appeal. But of course it is all very well to speak of simplicity; what matters is the kind of simplicity employed. What is required of a poet (it is everywhere implied in his writing), is a complete and total approach to the thing, an 'organically coordinated' approach. This involves an openness, a reverence, or shedding of preoccupations, ideas, theologies; even, perhaps, the theology of 'the thing'. In an essay on the Cork poet Seán Ó Ríordáin, first published in 1978, he writes of the way modern poets seem to be concerned with returning to (in George Steiner's phrase) the 'real presence' of things:

> It is as if they wished to experience anew man's first interaction with the material world without the intrusion of dogma or philosophy; to observe things as if we were the first generation on the planet.
>
> (*Repossessions*, p. 26)

Rainer Maria Rilke declared that he did not wish to express his own feelings, but 'things he had felt', with the emphasis on 'things'. 'Ceol Fómhair' ('Autumn Music') beautifully conveys the shock and surprise of total openness; in its dexterous and scrupulously attentive music, a way of looking as old as the earliest Irish lyrics is joined with a modern sensibility as advanced and free as that of the American poet William Carlos Williams. Paying attention at this pitch of receptivity is a discipline, a shearing away of all dogma and intellectuality to come to the thing itself. This arrival at a mood of total awareness is an act of the moral will but also pure gift; it is a recall of the pure outgoing of the spirit to the 'eternal Earth' in early Irish verse and it is also Ó Tuama, the individual, entirely there:

Is ceol téad im chluais
na duilleoga buí fáin
ag titim gan fuaim
ar an díon dearg stáin.

I hear string music
when stray yellow leaves
fall soundlessly down
on a red tin roof.

Speaking for myself, I find this more personal, because more formally achieved, than Williams's famous imagistic evocation of a red wheel-barrow:

So much depends
upon

a red wheel
barrow

glazed with rain
water

beside the white
chickens.

In the same Ó Ríordáin essay he quotes a gnomic statement of his friend: 'No one can taste his own taste', as if to say there can be no identity, no sense of self without a complementary recognition of something or someone other. Or, to recapitulate in the terms I've been using to site the artistic phenomenology of 'Ceol Fómhair', there can be no personally conceived and delivered utterance without some balancing tension obtaining between the individual perception and the matrices of tradition, community, language, and culture. This trembling interbalancing delivers living structure.

This consideration, if it be allowed, allows us to approach another feature of Ó Tuama's artistic method and consciousness, and one intimately bound up with his capacity to respond to the abrupt suddenness of things: it is what he calls, in the modestly-titled essay 'Three Lyrics I Like' (written in 1990), 'dramatic structure'. Patrick Pearse, in a lecture of 1912 entitled 'Some Aspects of Irish Literature' writes of the same or a similar quality which he finds in all phases of Irish literature, from the tenth-century *Serglige Con Culainn* (*The Wasting Sickness of Cú Chulainn*) to the near-contemporary lament for his dead son by Pádraig Ó hÉigeartaigh in the United States (the latter a poem which also fascinates Ó Tuama). Pearse describes this quality as a kind of force of utterance, 'the swift sure stroke at the very heart of *the thing*' (my italics). He also describes it as the 'clear detection of some naked truth'. It is precisely the task of unravelling this process of artistic, poetic, or literary detection that Ó Tuama sets himself as a critic, and this process he calls dramatic structure, whereby a complex human situation is entirely (or as near entirely as possible) comprehended and conveyed. As a poet, his more elaborately-structured works seek to situate emotion, personal feeling about things, in a fully-comprehended matrix of other materials, all organically coordinated in the dramatic impetus of realization.

Feeling and context are powerfully coordinated in the dramatic structure of 'Cá Siúlfam' (*Saol Fó Thoinn,* 1978). This is a poem of profound and lonely isolation, where the energy of life has ebbed very low. There may seem to be a contradiction here: how can a poet who so values being present to things write about alienation, about being *not* there to what is? How can a writer so convinced of the need to sing the actuality of existence (as in his Culdee-like sketches of Andros and Crete in his Greek poems), write of the breakdown of the connection between self and society, community, the natural world? Because the breakdown is itself part of the actuality, just as death is what gives impetus to life. Heidegger writes, in his seminal essay 'Das Ding' (1954), that death 'unveils the mountain range of being', or as the Jacobean John Donne has it, love and love of living is often 'begot' of 'absence, darkness, death/Things which are not'. So in 'Cá Siúlfam' we have what one might call a profound and dramatic structure which unveils the 'is not', and indeed there is a kind of exultant fortitude mixed with forbearance in the sincerity with which this personal emotion is linked to *absence* of community, the *absence* of consolation, religion, delight, even heat. The speaker is, by the end of his declaration, reduced to the thing he has become because of the absence of communication with another. 'My taste is me' wrote Hopkins in a similar mood of absence from his animate self. Ó Ríordáin says that no-one can taste himself, which may not strictly be true, because the entry into language itself, into structure and *its* animation means that the artist *may* be able to taste something like himself by means of his structure. Certainly 'Cá Siúlfam' has a taste, even if it is rank gall. But bitterness, celebrated, has its own tart savour.

Cá siúlfam? Tá na cosáin reoite,
carnáin chalcaithe de shneachta cruaite
ar bhlaincéadaí an bhóthair mar a mbíodh ár siúl.
'S tá an ghaoth ag aimsiú ioscada na nglún
chomh géar chomh glic le fuip . . . .
Ní shiúlfad leat. Tá an corp ina chloch.

Where shall we walk? The paths are all iced over;
on the grassy blankets of the roads we've known
calcified mounds of slush and snow.
The wind stings the hollows of the knees
as slyly and as sharply as a whip . . . .
I shall not walk with you. The flesh is stone.

To walk is to go together in communion. Ó Tuama quotes the psychiatrist Charles Rycroft who says that there is no one 'unless there are two men in communication', a remark of 1968, which, in its male-oriented perspective reveals something of the problem: it may be that alienation, because of the ferocity of male relationships, is something to which men are more susceptible than women. Whatever about this, the speaker in the poem refuses communication. The roads known are the familiar pathways of culture, order, civilization (an analogy at least as old as Montaigne), but in this dramatic unfolding they are places of suffering, exposure; the whip is present.

The second phase opens with a suitably ironical inflection. Alright then, if we will not walk, what about the car (shades of T.S. Eliot 'the closed car at four')? We can go to Mass:

Tiomáinfeam? Racham ar an aifreann déanach
ag éisteacht le Hosanna in Excelsis
á ghreadadh amach go buach caithréimeach,
is bainfeam sásamh as an at gan éifeacht
a thagann ar an gcroí . . . .
Chauffeur mé, lá seaca, ar dheabhóidí.

We shall drive then, go to Mass?
listen to Hosanna in Excelsis
being ground out triumphally,
and feed upon the silly satisfaction
of music swelling up the heart . . . .
On a frosty day I act as *chauffeur* to the mysteries.

A word about the Munster first person plural — 'siúlfam', 'racham' etc. — this also acquires an ironic inflection, as if to say, all the emotional pieties of collectivity, of the traditional, secure community of Cork, West Cork, the Muskerry Gaeltacht, are given a savage twist, as if to undercut the confident pertness of that lovely inclusive Munster plural. We are here in a singular universe, and yet, however ironically, that Munster world of family, father, loved ones, Doire an Aonaigh (where Ó Tuama spent time as a child) is still distantly, sadly, evoked by this laconic *chauffeur*, capable of luxuriating in that most vicious of sensualities, the religiose one, but knowing that all still remains as stone. Flesh remains stone, despite the false afflatus.

The final phase resists all movement, accepts the petrifaction, and waits. The *chauffeur* won't make himself absurd by going through the habits of routine; better stillness than the mendacity of going through the motions. Now the 'I' dominates; the plurals have all but receded; the dramatic process of the triumph of the solitary ego has been carried through to its chilling outcome:

> Ar deireadh: ní chorródsa amach inniu,
> tá fuil i gcúl mo bhéil le mí ón sioc,
> is ó inchinn go talamh síos
> tá bánú déanta ar gach artaire
> a dhéanann duine den daonaí . . . .
> Fanfam féach an bhfillfidh teas arís.
>
> No, just no: I will not move today.
> The chill has bloodied up my throat this long month past,
> and every artery that makes a human burn
> from brain down to the ground
> has been whitened to debility . . . .
> We'll wait and see if heat returns.

The anatomical petrifaction in the last stanza is much more convincing in the Irish. Ego has frozen everything up; however the Munster plural ('Fanfam') intrudes again at the end, as if to signify a faint tinkle of hope.

Here the dramatic structure of the poem, in its three deliberate phases, brings us to the 'heart of the thing', in Pearse's phrase, the thing here being a mood of sullen but helpless absence. The poem's vitality derives from the lived tension between the speaker's isolation and that full world out there, from which he is absent. In spite of the sophisticated knowingness the tone creates, the thing operates with a sincerity of utter desolation. The formality, the steady focus of the structure, keeps sentiment light-years away. It is, in its own way, a mordant celebration, a bleak dance of language and dramatic structure.

In the opening pages of *Repossessions*, in a brief background survey of Gaelic literary tradition and its contemporary flourishing, he focuses on a number of his central concerns as a writer and critic: describing two women poets, Áine Ní Ghlinn and Biddy Jenkinson, for instance, he says they have a 'poetic integrity', and that they express 'a completely individual sensibility'; the work of Michael Hartnett causes him to ruminate on the other pole of his balancing system, the need 'to achieve an overall definitive structuring of . . . subject matter'. The successful artist creates a living tension between these two concerns: structure and integrity.

Once, when I was a graduate student at UCC in the late 1960s, Ó Tuama, one day over a coffee told me of an exchange he'd had the previous summer while he had been at an international seminar at Harvard. He was at a cocktail party in Boston and an American lady asked him, as people do, what his 'field' was. Ó Tuama replied: 'My field? I suppose my field is love.' This, of course, strictly speaking, is true. He is the leading scholar of amatory tradition in Ireland, and an internationally recognized authority on courtly love, its conventions and psychologies, and the dissemination of its cult across Europe. He has written a couple of books on the topic: *An Grá in Amhráin na nDaoine* (1960) and *An Grá i bhFilíocht na nUaisle* (1988). These are works of literary history; they study how ideas and conventions migrate and modify; they discriminate between the ways in which a major creative talent engages with a body of thought and feeling; and how less gifted authors do not achieve a personal structuring of subject matter: the Ó Tuama weighing scales again.

But Ó Tuama is himself a very serious love poet, as in the opening section of *Saol Fó Thoinn*, represented in this selection by 'Cá Siúlfam' (its placing in a section devoted to poems of love in the collection gives its mordancy an added edge); 'Ise Seachtó hÓcht, Eisean Ochtó Ceathair'; 'An File dá Bhean', 'Cluiche'; and 'Amhrán Grá'.

'Cluiche' is a little piece of Catullan ferocity, as well as a bleak modernist evocation of erotic agony and violence. It conveys the damage wrought by passion; but it is no bleat of pain. The hurt and rage are given vent to by means of a strange and shocking symbolic phantasmagoria, which functions as the dramatic structure of the emotion. What, one asks, is the butler doing here? It is horrific, and conjoins mental and physical distress in a cold and surgical surrealism:

It was a quiet game with no knives:
she lighted up the desert all about her
and you submitted;
on a night of frost her pipers blew
a hundred welcomes in a spacious airport,
and you swelled up in tune;
but afterwards there came the shrinking:
her butler dragged you through narrow sewage pipes
and squeezed the vestiges of light from both your eyes.

Dali, Genet, *The Story of O*, all are here, as well as the reality of pain. What did this butler see? This is personal and marked by a 'distinctive' sense of individuality, but the writing is freed from the confusion and impediment of self-absorbed confession by the bold and scary imagery.

Love is not only, therefore, a matter of academic interest and searching enquiry in Ó Tuama; it is an obsession because it is a particularly intense manifestation of the ways in which people relate to each other in social formations. These formations themselves, Ó Tuama would (probably) argue, reflect that which, perhaps above all else, marks us out as a species – the instinct to create structures of relationship and difference. The lovers in 'Cluiche' are engaged in a 'love-game' of an especially vicious kind, but there is no doubt that what is being explored is the nature of a game in which it is possible for there to be as much rupture as there is 'at-one-ment'. What is not in doubt is the intensity of the central relation. (I am not for a moment necessarily implying that this is autobiographical in any vulgar or simplistic manner: intensity inheres in things which have been strongly felt, which is not to say that they have had, literally, to have happened.) This relation is one which is explored and re-enacted in the 'organically coordinated' (Corkery's phrase again) unfolding of the poem's structure: in other words the larger structures of the human mind and society are 'told', spelled out, shown, in the small animation that is the poem's life. Poetry and art are of profound value because they reveal to us what is eternal in human behaviour: those patterns and forms that subsist over and above (or under) the individual man or woman; those impulses that are the lineaments and strata of our minds, whereby we come close to an archaeology of consciousness itself. This archaeology of deep structures and alignments involves division and severance as much as cohesion and alliance. And the human behaviour of love is one arena, one game-play, where this whole system of relations is engaged in a very complex and personal manner. That and war. A poem of hatred and enmity, just as intense in its own way as 'Cluiche' is 'Trí Phictiúr dem Namhaid' ('Three Views of my Antagonist'), which is that rare thing, a poem welcoming open conflict, which recognizes hatred and disjunction as part of the complex structure of energy that animates society. Blake wrote truthfully of this, as has Francis Stuart in our time, but it is rare to find writers facing up to it in our era, probably because modern artists like to imagine themselves as liberals and civilized creatures. Not so here:

> I must set out in search of my antagonist:
> I value him more dearly than all my friends
> because he is vibrantly alive,
> and I carry dead flesh which will remain untried
> until we pull out our knives face to face.

However, it would be wrong to place too much emphasis on the discords in Ó Tuama's venturings into the complexity of human structures of relationship. There are serene and lovely poems of marriage and the pure gift of intimacy and (almost) untroubled oneness, as in 'Síos Linn':

> our feet at seabottom
> are glinting in sunlight.
> Let's jump up and down,
> move out of our depth,
> I'll bring you down with me,
> you'll surface back to me . . .

Love is one pattern of human behaviour which Ó Tuama has examined because it provides a particularly striking example of how personal feelings and instincts are implicated in larger social and cultural structures. Two other arenas of human relationships which also engage his creativity and intelligence are the family with its ties of kinship and filiation, and what may, loosely, be termed 'tradition' (though the Irish word 'dúchas' — which I would understand as 'hereditary core characteristics' — is more fitting), a repository of stored cultural memory which, in Irish, stretches back at least a millennium and a half. Each of these, family and tradition, are of course deeply implicated, the one with the other.

Ó Tuama's father came from the Muskerry Gaeltacht, and served as a judge in the alternative Sinn Féin courts during the War of Independence. His mother, whose brother was shot dead by Tans near the family home in Ballyvourney, saw active service (it seems) while teaching in Wexford. Childhood summers spent in Doire an Aonaigh and the surrounding areas, allowed Ó Tuama to absorb the cultural ethos and social mentality of this survival of the Gaelic world. The customs, outlook, and mind-set he encountered in Muskerry would have retained a vestigial contact with a culture and civilization that extended back past the Famine and Kinsale to strata and layers of conviction and persuasion that had embedded in them many of the modes and forms of early Irish culture and society: the emphasis on hospitality, the respect for children, the closeness of kinship ties, the interplay between pagan and Christian values, the sense that the otherworld was a potentially tactile reality; as well as the more negative aspects of a closed and narrow society, and one which saw its survival as dependent upon a struggle against English domination, and subsequently upon the arbitrary goodwill of the elected politicians of a new Free State. However, this world, as it appears in Ó Tuama's writings, tends not to be portrayed as narrow and life-denying, a depiction familiar to us from Frank O'Connor, say, or Máirtín Ó Cadhain. Ó Tuama is exercised without, I believe, any injustice to the facts of the situation, to show this world in a positive light on the whole because he perceives it as intimately bound up with family and kinship, concerns that elicit in him at least as much personal involvement as love.

A poem in *An Bás i dTír na nÓg* (1988), 'M'Athair' ('My Father'), memorializes an individual by presenting him as he was, but also by describing, in deeply affecting detail, how he represented a world of closeness and intimacy, that world of Muskerry in the 1930s from which he came and which he carried with him to Cork city and all over Munster where he worked as a travelling teacher of Irish. Once again personal feeling is developed and explored by means of a dramatic structure that moves lithely through the poem's various phases. Here is an extract in which the two men, the father and the uncle, are resting on the bog during turf-cutting. They both have blue eyes which have been 'generated by a long patient kindness/down the centuries amidst bare Muskerry mountains':

> I well remember him and Michael,
> two brothers, sitting on the bog,
> during the wartime shortages,

an idle *sleán* by each one's side,
and the four blue eyes dancing in unison.
The decorousness of those blue eyes
was their characteristic going right back . . .

The word 'characteristic' here is a poor translation of the word 'dúchas':

Suáilceas na súl gorm
b'shin é a dhúchas i bhfad siar.

Family, kinship, loyalty to one's own people: all these are themes accommodated in a spacious ode commemorating the house in which the family grew up in Cork, 'Maymount'. The closeness of these ties, lovingly and scrupulously evoked in the memory-bank the poem accumulates, moves curiously, and yet with a strange rightness, to a note of proud anger and disdain at the close, where the speaker says that all his efforts have been coordinated to issue a rebuke to those (plentiful in modern Ireland, it is implied) who would belittle the simplicity and goodness of his father and mother, burning turf and speaking Irish under the ornate gilt mirror in the old Victorian house. Ó Tuama is suggesting, very obliquely, that when push comes to shove, a family must close ranks:

. . . I won't allow upstarts
to belittle the two who made for me a little Eden
when turf was burning and talk was Irish under
  the gilt-framed mirror.

This leads me to the final point I want to make, concerning tradition, that other complex structure of Ó Tuama's. One can see in the above, I think, how familial affiliations and intimacies need to be protected: in other words, in societies where family and kinship are still highly valued, it is vitally necessary to have men (and women) brave enough to defend them and repel invaders ('allmhúraigh' in Irish, those 'beyond the walls', those who are exogamous). Such a closely-knit society needs heroes to protect its intimate secrecies and private sanctities. You need, in other words, a Christy Ring.

Ó Tuama's 'Pindaric Ode' of that title is one of his finest, wittiest, and most heart-breaking poems, calling before our eyes the great sportsman in all his vitality, tenderness, and miraculous glory. 'Ringy' is treasured because he is the valiant protector of the Cork secrecies and intimacies; his energy comes out of some hidden cauldron or reservoir of force that is pure tribal exhilaration. Ó Tuama's marvellous poem translates him from the 'Park' of a Sunday afternoon into a timeless dimension of myth and valour. Again the personal experience is given dramatic structure, in this case by the introduction of the airy speed of mythic time and space. The poem gives us a visceral jolt analogous to but different from what it 'felt like' to see Christy Ring in his glory:

In one moment of raw frenzy
as his playing days ran out,
he summoned Cú Chulainn
to aid him on the pitch:
his trunk swelled up
in sight of thousands,
one eye bulged
and danced, demented,
through clash and crash
hue and cry
men were toppled
hot blood spurted
and as he rammed in
three lethal goals
all the gods of ancient Ireland
lent his hurley a guiding hand.

The poem goes on to memorialize Christy Ring laid out on the slab of honour in the great tomb at Newgrange, cared for by Aengus, as the ray of light enters the inner chamber at the winter solstice. The poem thus affiliates the hero with the cycles of nature, those permanent forms. It may be 'likely that what is eternal is Earth not Man' but what Man and Woman know is death; they know it 'to the core' as Yeats says, and from that knowledge comes all art, all speech, all writing, all our deep structures.

Ó Tuama, as a writer, carries the authority of the man who has taken the trouble to know about death and celebrate life.

Sa bhliain 1995 bhronn Ollscoil na hÉireann an chéim D.Litt ar Sheán Ó Tuama, mar aitheantas ar a shaothar acadúil go speisialta. Tá sé tráthúil anois caoi a bheith againn díriú ar a shaothar cruthaitheach. Dá réir sin, fáiltím ó chroí roimh *Rogha Dánta, Death in the Land of Youth*.

Robert Welch
University of Ulster at Coleraine,
April 1997

Chronology

(Part-based on an interview in Cork, April 1997)

1926: Born in Blackpool, Cork to Aodh and Eibhlín (née Hegarty) Ó Tuama. Both had been active in the Republican movement.

1933: Family moved to 'Maymount', Gurranebraher, Cork and he began attending the Model School, Anglesea Street, an Irish-language school. Childhood summers were often spent at the paternal family home near Reananeree in the West Cork/Muskerry Gaeltacht.

1938: Began attending the Christian Brothers School, The North Monastery, Cork where he encountered a 'seminal' teacher, Pádraig Ó Callanáin.

1942: Entered University College, Cork (UCC), where he was taught English by Professor Daniel Corkery, a major influence.

1945: First Class Honours BA in Irish, Spanish, and English, coming first in the Faculty of Arts and taking first place in Ireland in the Mansion House Scholarship in Irish.

1946: First Class Honours MA in Irish.

1949: Appointed as Assistant Lecturer in the Department of Irish, UCC.

1950: Married Beití. Edited *Nuabhearsaíocht*, an anthology of modern verse in Irish with a critical introduction.

1955-6: Spent nine months in France studying contemporary theatre.

1959: PhD, *An Grá in Amhráin na nDaoine* (published 1960).

1961: Edition of *Caoineadh Airt Uí Laoghaire* (1961).

1962: *Faoileán na Beatha* (poems).

1965: Invited participant at the Harvard International Seminar run by Henry Kissinger.

1966: Visiting Professor at the Harvard Summer School. Publication of *Moloney* (plays).

1967: *Gunna Cam is Slabhra Óir* (play).

1968: Associate Professor of Irish, UCC.

1973: Editor *The Gaelic League Idea* (essays). Member of the Arts Council (until 1981).

1977: Visiting Research Professor, Jesus College, Oxford.

1978: *Saol Fó Thoinn* (poems).

1979: *Filí faoi Sceimhle* (study of Ó Ríordáin and Aogán Ó Rathaille).

1981: *An Duanaire: Poems of the Dispossessed* (with Thomas Kinsella).

1982-5: Chairman of Bord na Gaeilge until 1985.

1985: Professor Modern Irish Literature, UCC.

1988: *An Bás i dTír na nÓg* (poems).
An Grá i bhFilíocht na nUaisle (a study of courtly love in Gaelic aristocratic verse).

1990: *Cúirt, Tuath agus Bruachbhaile* (essays).

1995: *Repossessions* (essays on Irish literature translated from the Irish). Received a D.Litt (honoris causa) from the National University of Ireland.

1997: *Rogha Dánta/Death in the Land of Youth* (selected poems).

I

FUINNEOGA / WINDOWS

Fuinneoga '94

Mí Eanáir, lá ainnis liath,
d'oscail seal fuinneog sa spéir
is scaoileadh solas buí 'na shlaoda
anuas ar ghéaga fuara crann
faoina gclúmh donn gnéasach geimhridh,
is bhí cosán fionnuar órga ar an abhainn
ó bhruach go bruach im tharraingt
go críocha meala nach bhfuil ann.

Nuair d'oscail fuinneog bheag insa spéir
athuair an lá sin féin
shiúil scáil dhubh fir an cosán fionnuar
órga im threo go lúfar pras
siar isteach
im scornach.

Windows '94

A day in January, doleful, grey.
A window opened briefly
in the leaden clouds
and layers of yellow light
folded across the cold boughs
wrapped in an erotic brown fur
for winter, and a cool and golden path
stretched across the river
luring me to pastures sweet
(figments – I know, I know).

And later that same day
an even smaller window opened
and a man's black shadow
moving with purpose
approached me swiftly on the golden path
and quick-marched his way
down my gullet.

Ise Seachtó hOcht, Eisean Ochtó Ceathair

Nuair pósadh iad adúramar
'coinneoidh siad teas le chéile'
(ise caoga hocht, eisean seasca ceathair);
nuair cailleadh eisean, bhlaiseamar
an domlas 'nár mbéalaibh.

Ar dhéirc an stáit 'sea mhaireadar,
an tseanchaíocht a sólaist —
ach bhí aghaidh seanrí ársa anois
ar chorp a fir sa tseomra.

Liúigh sí le fíoch, do chuardaigh é
le méireanna páganta,
is sinne go críostaí ag guí
go gcoiscfí an sruth bolcánach.

Is ba bhaintreach ise ó oirthear domhain,
seál dubh is beol féasógach,
an t-aon bhean riamh lem mharthainse
a thit i ngrá le prionsa
(ise seachtó hocht, eisean ochtó ceathair).

She Being Seventy-Eight, He Being Eighty-Four

When they got married, we said
'They'll help to heat each other'
(she being fifty-eight, he being sixty-four).
When he passed away we felt
bile rising in our mouths.

They had lived on dole and grants,
gossip their one solace –
but the dead face in the room now
was of an old king from the past.

She shrieked with rage, and combed him
with pagan fingerings,
while we sound Christians prayed
that the lava-flow would stop.

She looked a widow of the Eastern world,
black shawl and moustached mouth,
the only woman in my lifetime
to have loved a prince
(she being seventy-eight, he being eighty-four).

An File dá Bhean

(*as an dráma* Corp Eoghain Uí Shúilleabháin)

Oíche lán de cheatha beaga ar dhúiseacht dom,
casaim chūghat is chím le léire iontasach
gur strainséar coirp tú sínte síos le sliasaid liom,
is áthasaíonn an t-ainmhí istigh ionam.

Ach sé dúrt liom féin aréir 's an spéir amuigh á scoilt
(is an t-ainmhí simplí istigh faoi scanradh ionam):
'dá bhfaighfeá bás anois
do leáfadh náire mé.'
Níl ansin adeir mo chiall inniu le gaois
ach seana-nath gan bhrí.
Cuireann an duine daonna de formhór gach ní . . . .
Fós, thuig mo chroí aréir gur náire follasach
nár mhó ná strainséar riamh bhí liom chun cónaithe,
gur lú tar éis na mblian mo thuiscint ort,
ná ar athair is deartháir is daoine muinteartha
nár mhalartaíos sa tsaol seo riamh ach focail leo.
'Níor mhaite d'éinne' (adúrt), 'faillí chomh coirpeach san!'

Ach gan mhoill 'na dhiaidh sin scoir na toirneacha amuigh,
is bhís chomh te teolaí, strainséartha, lán de chion,
gur áthasaigh an t-ainmhí arís istigh ionam.

The Poet to His Wife

(*from the play,* Corp Eoghain Uí Shúilleabháin)

A night of light persistent showers when I awake,
I turn towards you and see in wonderment
a stranger, motionless, laid out by my side,
and the animal within me leaps, elatedly.

But last night as thunder split the sky
(and the animal within cowed low in misery)
I said, 'If you, my wife this moment died
shame would melt my heart and limbs.'
Today, of course, my reason jibs
at cosmic clichés of the kind.
A human being, I know, survives most things.
Yet, last night, my heart realized the melting shame
of having kept you as a stranger in my territory,
someone who after all those years I know much less
than father, mother, brothers, relatives –
who in this life exchange but words with me.
'Neglect like this' I told myself,
'is bred out of barbarity.'

But when the rumble in the sky had lost its potency,
and you my stranger wife beside me, soft and full of tenderness,
the animal in me leaped up again for ecstasy.

Cá Siúlfam?

Cá siúlfam? Tá na cosáin reoite,
carnáin chalcaithe de shneachta cruaite
ar bhlaincéadaí an bhóthair mar a mbíodh ár siúl.
'S tá an ghaoth ag aimsiú ioscada na nglún
chomh géar chomh glic le fuip . . . .
Ní shiúlfad leat. Tá an corp ina chloch.

Tiomáinfeam? Racham ar an aifreann déanach
ag éisteacht le Hosanna in Excelsis
á ghreadadh amach go buach caithréimeach,
is bainfeam sásamh as an at gan éifeacht
a thagann ar an gcroí . . . .
Chauffeur mé, lá seaca, ar dheabhóidí.

Ar deireadh: ní chorródsa amach inniu,
tá fuil i gcúl mo bhéil le mí ón sioc,
is ó inchinn go talamh síos
tá bánú déanta ar gach artaire
a dhéanann duine den daonaí . . . .
Fanfam féach an bhfillfidh teas arís.

Where Shall We Walk?

Where shall we walk? The paths are all iced over;
on the grassy blankets of the roads we've known
calcified mounds of slush and snow.
The wind stings the hollows of the knees
as slyly and as sharply as a whip . . . .
I shall not walk with you. The flesh is stone.

We shall drive then, go to Mass?
listen to Hosanna in Excelsis
being ground out triumphally,
and feed upon the silly satisfaction
of music swelling up the heart . . . .
On a frosty day I act as *chauffeur* to the mysteries.

No, just no: I will not move today.
The chill has bloodied up my throat this long month past,
and every artery that makes a human burn
from brain down to the ground
has been whitened to debility . . . .
We'll wait and see if heat returns.

Siúlóid in Éirinn

(do Bheití in aois a seasca sé)

Tar éis dúinn faobhar na faille a ghabháil
trí sceacha is trí dhraighean
— láib ar ár mbróga, méirscrí ar ár lámha —
nocht geata dearg péinteáilte romhainn
ar leaca gharbh goirt
is dúrtsa leat go cleithmhagúil
(is stailc bheag dhubh im chroí)
'ní mheallfaidh tú go deo mé
ón mbóthar mór arís'.
Ansin sea sceinn éan mór breacórga
de na sreanga os ár gcionn
is lean mionchleitearnach 'nár dtimpeall seal
ar thonntracha an aeir.
Láithreach bonn ina dhiaidh sin
d'éirigh péasún sa bhféar fada
is do rop ina árthach dorcha donn
ag iomramh tríd an spéir.

Leanfad tamall eile
tríd an ngairfean tú, a chroí;
bíonn éin órga go coitianta
ar tinneall os do chionn,
is éiríonn péasúin ag do chosa
pé áit a mbíonn do shiúl.

A Walk in Ireland

(for Betty on her sixty-sixth birthday)

We had made it by the cliff-edge
through thorn trees and briars,
mud on our shoes, hands chapped and scarred,
when a red painted gate appeared
on the rough field's slope,
and I said teasingly to you –
masking a certain sulkiness of heart –
'you will never again deflect me
from the safe highway'.
Just then a speckled golden bird
fled off the wires overhead
(the flutter of its wings lingering
on the surrounding air-waves)
and within an instant a pheasant rose
from the long wild grasses –
a brown-black vessel coursing
fiercely through the skies.

I'll follow you a little longer love
through the rough stony places:
for golden birds do commonly
vibrate above your head
and pheasants rise at your feet
wherever you care to walk.

Rousseau na Gaeltachta

Lig di, adúirt an file,
is ná smachtaigh í,
níl inti seo ach gearrchaile
is is breoiteacht é an t-eagla
a chrapann an nádúr.

Lig di, adúirt an file,
is ná smachtaigh í,
lig di fás gan bac ar bith
go dtína hairde cheapaithe:
tá an t-aer fós bog os a cionn.

A Gaeltacht Rousseau

Let her be, said the poet
do not chastise her,
she is still a stripling
and fear is a sickness
that stunts all human growth.

Let her be, said the poet
do not chastise her,
let her grow unimpeded
to whatever height she is meant for:
the air is still soft above her head.

Christy Ring

Do thriail sé an ní dodhéanta
formhór gach Domhnach ar an bpáirc,
is uaireanta rith leis.

Ar leathghlúin dó,
teanntaithe i gcúinne,
nuair las a shúil —
réamhchríostaí, leictreonach —
's gur dhiúraic an liathróid uaidh
thar trasnán,
chrith an t-aer le hiontas.

Nuair thug gan coinne
aon ráig ghlan fiain
trí bhulc na bhfear
's gur phléasc an sliotar
faoi smidiríní solais
sa líontán,
do liúigh an laoch
san uile dhuine.

Aon neomat buile amháin
in earr a ré
is é Cúchulainn
bhí 'na ionad
ar an bpáirc:
d'at a chabhail
i radharc na sluaite,
do bholgaigh súil
's do rinc ar mire,
bhí cnagadh is cleatar,
liútar-éatar,
fir á dtreascairt,
fuil ag sileadh —

Christy Ring

He aimed at the impossible
each Sunday on the pitch;
sometimes he succeeded.

Down on one knee,
trapped in a corner of the field,
when his prechristian electronic eye
lit up in combat,
and the ball, a missile,
sped from him straight above the bar,
the air shook in awe.

When a driving lunge
brought him clear beyond
the ruck of men,
and the ball, propelled,
self-destructed in the net
to smithereens of light,
our cheering became a battle cry.

In one moment of raw frenzy
as his playing days ran out,
he summoned Cú Chulainn
to aid him on the pitch:
his trunk swelled up
in sight of thousands,
one eye bulged
and danced, demented,
through clash and crash
hue and cry
men were toppled
hot blood spurted

’s nuair rop trí cúil isteach
bhí seandéithe Éireann uile
ag stiúrú a chamáin.

Dúirt bean os cionn a choirp
tráth a bháis anabaidh:
‘ba mhór an peaca é
an fear san a adhlacadh’.

Ní féidir liomsa fós
Christy Ring a adhlacadh . . . .
Samhlaím é uaireanta
is é ar buanchoimeád,
sínte ar leac na honóra
i mBrú na Bóinne
is Aonghas Mac an Daghda á choimhdeacht
go dtí an leath-uair bheag gach geimhreadh
go soilsíonn ga gréine go hómósach
ar a chúntanós.

Ach ní fhéadfadh aoinne againne
a mhair faoi bhriocht ag Christy Ring
é leagadh uainn go buan faoi ghlas
i measc míorúiltí na seanmhiotas —
mar, ó na míorúiltí
chonaiceamar dáiríre
is a chúntanós faoi loinnir
formhór gach Domhnach
geimhreadh is samhradh
ar an bpáirc.

and as he rammed in
three lethal goals
all the gods of ancient Ireland
lent his hurley a guiding hand.

Looking at his corpse laid out,
the day of his untimely death,
a woman said:
'It would be a sin to bury such a man.'

I have not managed yet to bury Christy Ring.
Sometimes I imagine him
being venerated
in the care of the great god, Aengus,
on a slab at Newgrange
and at each winter solstice
for just one half an hour
a ray of sunshine
lighting up his countenance.

But no friend of his could think
of laying Christy Ring eternally to rest
locked in with ancient miracles –
for oh the miracles of the living flesh
we saw when his countenance lit up
winter days and summer days,
Sundays in and Sundays out,
on the playing pitch.

An Cat

Na míosa roimh a bás
ní raibh fhios aici go cruinn
aon neomat beag amháin
cá luífeadh nó cá rachadh sí:
í sínte, teanntaithe, ar chlabhar,
í neadaithe fiarsceabhach sna leabhair
nó á ruagairt don raidió.
Do lobhaigh gan stad a clúmh
is do shil go fras ribí
ar bhoird is ar éadaí.
Ansin d'imigh uainn faoi rún
faoi mar a bhraithfeadh sí
doicheall éigin inár gcroí —
go bhfuarthas 'na búrla lofa í
i ngaráiste comharsan.

Ní raibh inti is dócha
ach gnáthchat dubh,
ach ba mheasa le bean a' tí
í dhul uainn i gcré
ná scrios na Traoi
nó, fiú, bás obann Christy Ring.
Níorbh iad na déithe ná na laochra
ba chás léi sin,
ach an cat beag dubh bhí lán de chion,
an peata deireanach insa tigh.

The Cat

Months before she died,
she never really knew
where to wander or lie down
at any given time –
stretched on the mantelpiece, hemmed in,
nestling amongst books askew
or being hunted off the radio.
Her fur fell away,
she left tufts everywhere
on tables and chairs
then quit us silently
as if she had sensed some disaffection
brooding in our hearts –
and afterwards was found a bundle rotting
in a neighbour's garage.

She rated no more perhaps
than any ordinary black cat,
but her passing left a deeper mark
on the lady of the house
than the tragic sack of Troy
or even the sudden death of Christy Ring.
Her concern was not at all
the deeds of heroes or of gods –
but her little black cat so full of love
the last pet in the house.

Maymount: Tigh Victeoireach a Leagadh

Thíos faoin scáthán leathan imeall-órga haut-bourgeois
bhíodh m'athair is mo mháthair seal den oíche suite,
iad á mbuanú féin tar éis blianta na trioblóide,
an sciathóg móna 's an tlú fada ag a gcosa.
Bhíodh móin á dó is Gaeilge á labhairt faoin scáthán imeall-órga.

Do bhuanaigh siad iad féin sa lomathigh scóipiúil Victeoireach
(de réir mar a bhuanaigh an Stát nua é féin sa tír):
péiríní buí san úllord nár chleacht a muintir rompu,
cnag aitheanta camán sa ghairdín cúil.
Bhí réimeas úr sa tsiúl ar chliatháin bhaile mhóir Chorcaí.

Mhúin mo mháthair dúinn an dul chun cinn, an mhatamaitic,
thál m'athair an tseanaimsearthacht, an dul chun cinn ar gcúl;
cibeal laethúil tí mhóir, cártaí is polaitíocht —
is nead againn sa tSamhradh ar thalamh portaigh Mhúscraí.
Do labhair treabhchaisí na dúiche sin 'nár gcluasa-ne de shíor.

Earrach amháin scaoil m'athair sreang ar sheanagheata iata
is b'shiúd romhainn i measc ár mbráithre cathrach ar an gcnoc,
bheannaíodar dúinn 'na mBéarla grámhar Gaelach
is cheangail roinnt againn ár ndílseacht leo go buan.
(Ach gibris ba theanga súgartha ag beirt óg anois den chlann.)

Leath amhras ag an am ná raibh an Stát de réir a bhriathair —
tréas imeartha ar ár muintir ghaibhnithe ó thuaidh —
bhí náire follas trína mórtas ar mo mháthair
as an mbonn óir ghnóthaigh as a laochas sa Réabhlóid.
Is bhí piléir an IRA faoi sna háirsí san úllord.

An mac ba shine againn bhí thíos le híogair-racht na treibhe
(oidhre a úncail d'fhág Dúchrónaigh sínte i ndíg);
tharraingíomar bia chuige sa bheairic laethe gréine —
é faoi ghlas ag Éireannaigh 'na chathair féin.
'S ní fhacamar 'na shláinte é arís go deireadh a shaoil.

Maymount: a Victorian House, Demolished

Under the wide gilt-framed mirror, haut-bourgeois,
my mother and father sat at evening time,
settling in after the years of the troubles,
with a basket of turf and the fire-tongs standing by.
Turf was burnt as they talked in Irish under the gilt-framed mirror.

They settled into the spacious Victorian residence
(much as the new State settled into the land);
an orchard of golden pears brought a new delicious taste,
the old sounds of hurling were heard behind the house.
A fresh regime had started up on the steep streets of Cork.

My mother taught us to get ahead, mathematics,
my father gave us old ways, progressing through the past;
the usual big family fussing, card-games, politics —
and our summer home in Muskerry's soft boglands.
There the people's past spoke constantly in our ear.

One springtime my father loosed the tie on the old gate
and let us out among our city playmates on the hill,
they greeted us in their warm Irish-English
and we took to each other in comradeship
(Although two of our youngsters took to gibberish for their fun.)

At that time suspicion grew amongst us
that the State had abandoned our people in the North,
my mother's delight was pierced with shame
for her War of Independence prized gold medal.
And the IRA stored ammunition in the orchard walls.

The eldest son inherited the anger of his people
(heir of an uncle laid low in a dyke by Tans).
We took him food in the barracks on summer days
kept under lock and key by Irishmen in his own city.
He never recovered health again.

Do lean faoi sheol seal eile fós na gnáthimeachtaí clainne,
ceoladh, pósadh, líon leanaí an tigh arís:
ní sliocht réabhlóide bhí chun té anois sa chistin
ach sliocht mar chách ar mhór leo ualach a lae féin.
'S ba lú den Ghaeilge a chloistí anois faoin scáthán imeall-órga.

Do chríon an seanathigh de réir mar chríon an tseanamhuintir,
thit slintreacha, scoilt píopaí, bhí sileadh i seomra an ghuail;
ba pháis dom mháthair é an seomra in airde a shroichint,
áit ar saolaíodh clann di, is go gcaitheadh súil bainríona
uaithi síos ar spící teampall 's ar longa i gcuan Chorcaí.

An lá aistríomar iad dúirt comharsa mná 'God love them'
(an casadh deireanach eochrach sea ghoin a croí);
'na gcónaí nua fuair freastal is ómós gan choimse —
ach bhí fraitheacha na beatha cúngaithe orthu anuas.
'S nuair réabadh a bpálás Victeoireach níor nocht os ard a
gcumha.

(Is eolach domhsa anois go gcaitheann daoine a bpurgadóireacht
in árasáin nár taibhríodh riamh ar aon réabhlóid,
i seomraí cúnga nár saolaíodh is nár throid aon leanbh,
áit gurb aithris gach gáire ar gháire a bhí ann cheana,
's go mbíonn balaithe múin stálaithe de shíor id shróin.)

Tar éis a báis do chuimhníos lá gan choinne ar mo mháthair,
in Oaxaca, cathair ghréine i Meicsiceo,
nuair chonac uaim i bplásóg ghreanta Spáinneach suite —
na geal-uaisle ag gabháil thairsti gan í fheiscint —
Indiach maorga mná 's í faid gach n'fhaid 'na staic ag feitheamh.

Mar sin laethe bhíodh mo mháthairse i Maymount suite
is pléisiúr ársa éigin ar a cúntanós,
a ceannaithe go mómharach, gan bhuairt, gan bhogadh,
is í, i ngan fhios di féin, ag feitheamh is ag feitheamh
chun go dtiocfadh slán ó gach anró an treabh dar di í.

The usual round of family things continued,
sing-songs, weddings, and children in the house again:
no rebels having tea in our kitchen now
but a rising generation making its own way.
And little Irish to be heard now under the gilt-framed mirror.

The old house showed its age just like the old couple,
slates fell, pipes burst, there was a drip in the coal-store;
my mother struggled upstairs to the room in which
her children had been born, and from where she used
to look down on Cork — its spires, and berthed ships.

The day we moved them out a neighbour said 'God love them'
(that last twist of the key pierced the heart);
in their small apartment they had every thing they needed —
but now the walls of their lives were closing in on them.
And they showed no grief when Maymount was demolished.

(Now I know that people live their purgatory
in places where no one dreams of revolution,
in narrow rooms where children were never born or quarrelled,
places where each laugh only shadows bygone laughter,
where the smell of stale piss is for ever in your nose.)

After she died I remembered my mother suddenly
one day in Oaxaca, a sunlit city in Mexico,
when in a gravelled Spanish square, I saw —
ignored by the bright and beautiful who passed her by —
a majestic Indian woman who simply sat stock-still.

That was how my mother was most days in Maymount,
sitting transfixed by some ancient pleasure,
her features stately, easy, steadfast,
and herself, unknowing, waiting and waiting
until her people came safely through all hardship.

Is sa mhéid gur chuireas féin chun cinn go poiblí, nó
príobháideach,
an t-athaoibhneas a shantaigh m'athair is í féin,
is chuige é, cuid mhaith, ná leomhfainn do bhoicíní
fonóid faoi bheirt a chuir sna flaithis bheaga mé
tráth bhí móin á dó is Gaeilge á labhairt faoin scáthán imeall-
órga.

Bás Fómhair

Sa bhfómhar a d'éag sí i dtús séasúir an tseaca.
Is cuimhin liom fós im aigne nárbh fheasach
d'éinne againn,
ná fiú di féin, an bás a bheith ag fáscadh
leis go láidir ina cliabh. Mhaisigh
sí a tigh,
phioc blátha sa ghairdín, chuir vásaí dú
criadóra ar chlabhar marmair go grástúil —
ansan gan coinne
d'imigh sa tsíoraíocht, is í 'na gearrchaile.
Dhein a bás, ar nós an tseaca,
lot is milleadh;
ach 'na dhiaidh, do bheoigh niamh gach datha
is cumhrachtaí an fhómhair.

And if, in public or in private, I myself advanced
the joyful renewal that my parents wished for,
it's mostly that I won't allow any upstarts
to belittle the two who made for me a little Eden
when turf was burning and talk was Irish under the gilt-framed
    mirror.

Elegy on the Death of a Young Married Woman

She died in autumn just as the frosts began.
None of us had known that death
quite casually was operating near her heart.
She cared for her house, set flowers,
placed vases of black pottery on her marble chimney-piece
with a certain unprovincial style.
And then quite suddenly passed straight into eternity.
Her death, like autumn frost, ravaged every life within its reach.
But afterwards
the hue of every colour
in eye on face on tree on river
burned right down through the brain
and the fragrances of autumn leaped everywhere.

Abair do Phaidir

(an tan a rinne polaiteoirí tréas ar náisiúntóirí na hÉireann)

Abair do phaidir (más cuimhin leat í),
ná bac an té adéarfaidh leat
nach cóir gach lá guí ar son
ár muintire a dhein foréigean
nuair ab éigean dóibh.

Anseo ar ché na Gaillimhe
i measc seantán is tithe stórais,
i measc fo-éadaí ag sileadh súlaigh,
tá greanta ar sheanchloch tréigthe an scríbhinn:
'guigh ar son anam uasal x
a fuair bás ar son na saoirse'.
Ná múch anois ionat an phaidir
a líonann ort aniar-aduaidh.

Dhein x foréigean, ní foláir –
agus dhein fir a pháirte roimhe:
dheineadar, le binb,
pící a ropadh
piléir a ghreadadh
cnámha a bhriseadh
scornaigh a ghearradh,
is súile boga a phiocadh
as a log sa chloigeann –
  d'fhonn teacht slán.

Abair do phaidir go simplí nádúrtha
ar son daoine a bhí iad féin nádúrtha,
is a chleacht foréigean de réir a ngnáis.
Iarr ar an Dia is ansa leat
ná fágfaí iad anois ar crochadh
gan ómós ná aithint choiteann
i measc fo-éadaí is fallaí gruama
de dheascaibh tréas na bpolaiteoirí . . . .
Is barbair bhunaidh iad aon chine

Say a Prayer

(at a time when Irish politicians broke faith with their ancestors)

Say a prayer (if you remember any)
don't mind all those who tell us
it is politically incorrect to pray
for those before us who took to violence
when only violence was on offer.

On this derelict Galway quayside
in the jumble of sheds and buildings
under the drip from a line of clothes
you will find a worn slab engraved:
'Pray for the noble soul of X
who died in the fight for freedom.'
Clear a way for that insistent prayer
which takes you a little by surprise.

X was, no doubt, a violent man,
violent, too, his people.
With deadly purpose
they stuck with pikes,
blasted with shot,
smashed bones,
severed throats,
and gouged soft eyes
from the sockets
all to survive.

Say your prayer, intimately, naturally,
for people who themselves were naturally
violent in the political correctness of their age.
Plead with the God you cherish
not to leave them drifting there
unrecognised, despised,
between dank walls and dripping clothes
because our politicians abandon them.
It is against all nature to deny

ná tugann an t-ómós is dual
don saghas foréigin is dual ómós
ó tháinig ann don duine.

Abair do phaidir, fiú más í
do phaidir, um a' dtaca seo,
do dheor.

Cluiche

Ba chluiche ciúin gan sceana é:
do shoilsigh sí an fásach ina timpeall féinig
agus ghéillis;
nuair a shéid a píobairí
céad fáilte romhat in aerfort fairsing oíche sheaca d'atais;
ach ina dhiaidh sin d'ordaigh sí tú chrapadh,
is dhein a buitléir tú tharraing trí phíobáin chúnga múnlaigh
féach an bhfáiscfí rian gach solais as do shúile.

homage to that violence
which has been honoured
since we became human.

Say your prayer – even if
you find your prayers
have turned to tears.

Love-Game

It was a quiet game with no knives:
she lighted up the desert all about her
and you submitted;
on a night of frost her pipers blew
a hundred welcomes in a spacious airport,
and you swelled up in tune;
but afterwards there came the shrinking:
her butler dragged you through narrow sewage pipes
and squeezed the vestiges of light from both your eyes.

Rince Seite

(*cois tuama Naomh Proinsias in Assisi, Aibreán, 1991*)

Is é údar mór mo cheana ort le ceart
gur fear tú a raibh comrádaithe agat
(ní hionann is na fáidhithe ón seanreacht,
aonaráin a labhraíonn leo *ex cathedra*).
As t'óige amach bhí páirtithe led chois,
ag fiach, ag bruíon, ag suirí ar an gcnoc,
is nuair a thugais-se fé dheoidh na móide
a bheith id gheocach ag Dia na Glóire
choinnigh roinnt den bhuíon sin ceol leat,
d'éist siad leis na héin is leis na lobhair
is dhein fo-chéim mheisciúil rince i gan fhios;
agus, ar deireadh thiar, do mhaisigh duit
an tsíleáil scléipeach 'tá ag glioscarnaigh
le dúthracht sa doircheacht, i d'Eaglais
os mo chionn. Do hadhlacadh le haimsir
iad súd ba ghile leat ded bhráithre
anseo thíos in uaimh faoi thalamh: iad cruinnithe
i gciorcal timpeall ar do chomhrainn
ag súil le haiséirí id theannta.

Táim féin go mór in amhras an éireoidh sibh.
(Fós labhraíonn gach tuama liom anseo
go húdarásach ar bhuaine an charadais
is ar scarúint shealadach compánach. . . .)

Proinsias, Rufus, Luca is aroile,
éirigí de hap in éineacht!
Beannacht Dé chũghaibh níl agaibhse
ach bhur lámha a shíneadh amach i dtreo
a chéile. Beir isteach air, a Phroinsias,
fáisc do bhráthair — céim bheag ruthaig,
gread an clár, is siúd sa timpeall
rincí seite ag cnagarnaigh
ar urláir uile na síoraíochta.

Set Dance

(at the crypt of Saint Francis in Assisi, April 1991)

My liking for you is easily accounted for –
you were a man who revelled in good company
(unlike the solitary patriarchs of yore
who spoke – when spoken to – *ex cathedra*).
From childhood you were always with your friends,
out hunting, fighting, courting on the hills;
then later when you took a solemn vow
to be a juggler in the service of the Lord
your gang of friars joined in the music-making
and helped you listen to the birds and lepers
and also (if it was called for) danced.
Before the end they painted here for you
the merry motley-coloured ceiling
which glistens fervently in the gloom
of your basilica high above me.
The best loved of your brethren now
lie buried hereabouts in this crypt
gathered in an arc about your tomb
and with you wait for resurrection day.

If you ask me, I greatly doubt that any of you
will rise again (though every tomb I see
sings of the certainty of lasting friendship
and a sure end to earthly parting).

Come on now,
Francis, Rufus, Luca and the rest of you,
rise up at once together.
Glory be, just reach
your hands out to each other.
Grab him, Francis, hug him,
rap the boards and you're away
with all the untiring set-dancers
across Heaven's busy floor.

Coinní Iarbháis

Tar éis a báis
do bhí sí romhat
ag gach cúinne sráide,
í ar leathghlúin, nocht,
ag casachtaigh
is riasta dearg gránna
mar a mbíodh cíoch léi
ar a bráid.
Ba bhean í, is fíor, thar mhná —
ach ní chothaíonn na mairbh grá:
scrios a huimhir teileafóin
go pras ded dhialann
is éirigh as coinní iarbháis.

Assignations with the Dead

After she died
she appeared to you
at every turning of the street,
naked, on one knee,
coughing and distraught,
an ugly red wound
where her breast had been.
True she was a woman apart
but the dead cannot nourish a living need:
cross out her number
promptly from your diary
and give up your assignations with the dead.

Ag na Soilse Dearga

(i bParis)

An cailín sa chóta fearthainne
a bhfuil an clogad ar a ceann
chím í ag na soilse dearga,
dealbhaithe sa cheofrán trom.

Foighníonn sí le neamhchaise
ar chúlaibh inneallrothair nua,
an aghaidh Rómhánach ghreanta aici
go geal 'na tost san oíche chrón.

Ansan gan aon tsamhailt dithnis
claonann sí a ceann chun cinn,
's an té atá ar bhéalaibh tuigeann sé
is claonann seisean chuici siar.

Is an phóg amháin, le cineáltas,
a chuir go héadrom ar a bheol,
ní raibh mian an choirp ná toirt inti
's níor bhearnaigh snáth dá cochall ceoigh.

An solas glas! D'aon léim amháin
stracann sruth tormáin mo mheabhair,
's, gan bhrí, sa tranglam gluaisteán,
tá sí slogaithe as m'amharc . . . .

Ba mhéadú croí bheith roimpi arís
ag an gcéad chrois eile go maolóidh
gleithearán an tráchta diaidh ar ndiaidh . . .
's ansan, mar shacraimint, an phóg.

At the Red Lights in Paris

The girl in the mackintosh
with a helmet on her head
I see her at the red lights
sculptured in the heavy fog.

She waits, a practised pillion-rider,
on a humming motor-bike,
her shapely silent Roman face
shining in the tawny night.

With no hint of haste or flurry
she bends forward from her seat
and her alert front-rider
bends backwards to her lips.

The one kiss of tenderness
she laid lightly on his lips
had neither desire or density
and left her cowl of fog intact.

The green light! In one crashing burst
a stream of noise floods through my brain
and absurdly in a mass of cars
she has vanished out of sight.

I'd dearly love to reach before her
the next red traffic lights on this hill,
to hear the engines slow to idle
– and then the sacramental kiss.

Beannacht Abhaile

Toisc gur tú a nochtaigh sceinne-chroí an tsaoil dom,
scaip ceannabhán sa ghaoith an t-am ba lú mo shúil,
chun ná ligfí i ndearmhad comaoin príntísigh —
cuirim an bheannacht so ar bharraicíní chūghat.

Toisc gur tú, de shíor, a fhulaingíonn ár n-áthas,
's go bhfulaingíonn tú anois arís é go grástúil,
tá sreanga m'anama ar crith dhuit le cineáltas —
is cuirim an bheannacht so ar shreang cineáltais chūghat.

Is toisc go gcloisfimídne arís i mbéal trá báine
uisce ag sileadh i ngoile carraigreacha dúr
(istigh fén leac ghéar dhubh éist! féach! leanaí ag gáirí) —
ó cuirim an bheannacht so ar ghaethe gréine chūghat.

Greetings from Abroad

Because it was you who quickened in me the pulse of living,
scattered bog-cotton on the wind when my hopes ran low,
to honour the outstanding debt of an apprentice
I send these greetings on tiptoes to you.

Because it is you who continually endures our pleasure
(and endures it once again with uncomplaining ease)
my soulstrings are trembling with new tenderness –
I send these greetings on a string of tenderness to you.

And because we both shall hear again through a white strand's
music
water dripping in the maw of recalcitrant cliff-rocks
(under the black rock's sloping see! hear! children laughing)
I send these greetings on sunlit rays to you.

Asailín Pharis

(do dhaoine óga)

Do ghluais sé tríd an margadh,
an t-asailín beag dubh,
's má ghluais, do ghluais mar asailín
gur ghradam leis a chros.

Níor bhrúigh sé trísna sluaite cruinn,
níor shatail ar aon chois,
ach d'fhan ar nós duine uasailín
gur deineadh cosán do.

Bhí cloigín ar a éadan umhal
faoi shíoda dearg tláth;
ba shéipéal sásta an sráidín cúng
is é ag gabháil thar bráid.

D'fhair gach súil go haislingiúil
an ciseán ar a dhrom,
d'íslíodh gach srón le mórchathú
nuair d'imigh sé as amharc.

Mar níorbh ainmhí chun ualaigh so,
ná asal móna groí,
ag díol snaoisín labhandair
bhí asailín Pharis.

The Little Paris Donkey

(for young people)

He stepped up through the market square,
the donkey small and black,
he stepped along, quite proud to wear
the cross upon his back.

He did not shoulder through the press,
nor stood on any feet,
but stopped and paused – *quelle politesse* –
until they cleared the street.

A tinkling bell with red silk bound
was hanging at his head
and worship followed him around
everywhere he went.

The people stared with dreamy sight
at the basket that he bore,
their nostrils flared with lost delight
when he was seen no more.

Not bred for work in rough terrain
or to be a beast of burden,
he carried lavender for sale,
this little Paris donkey.

Amhrán Grá

(*as an dráma* Iúdás Iscariot agus a Bhean)

Tá Dia ar lár a anam liom,
  gráimís a chéile;
níl maith ar bith san aifreann,
  adhraimís a chéile.

Tá cloig na dteampall beannaithe
  ag gliogarnach gan éifeacht,
fill gan mhoill a anam liom
  is ceolfaimid le chéile.

'S mura bhfuil aon ghrá eadrainn,
  'S gur ag ligint orainn a bhímíd,
ligimís orainn tamall fós
  nó alpfaimíd a chéile.

The Musician's Love-Song

(*from a play* Iúdás Iscariot agus a Bhean)

God is dead my lovely one,
let us love each other,
mass has been said my lovely one,
let's adore each other.

The bells of all the churches
are jingling with no purpose,
return to me my lovely one
and we'll make proper music.

And if we find there is no love,
that we are just pretending,
let's pretend another while
or we'll devour each other.

Trí Phictiúr dem Namhaid

Is é seo go cruinn mo namhaid:
mangaire líofa na bhfocal teibí –
an ceart, an fhírinne, an chríostaíocht –
is satlann ar dhaoine go teann.

Is é seo arís mo namhaid:
saoithín mion ag abhcóidíocht –
údar tur te ón síoraíocht -
's, ar an dímheas doimhin 'na thimpeall, dall.

Ach is é seo bunchló mo namhad:
aighneasóir ar gharbh leis comhrac claímh,
a sheargaigh 's a chuaigh i laghad,
's gur imigh an nimh 'na pheann.

Ní mór dom bualadh amach ag lorg mo namhad,
is mó agamsa é ná a bhfuil de chairde agam ar domhan,
mar tá sé 'na steilleabheathaidh,
is feoil mharbh orm féin ná preabfaidh
go nochtfaimid na sceana, bonn le bonn.

Three Views of my Antagonist

This is precisely my antagonist:
an eloquent purveyor of abstract nouns –
justice, truth and christian charity –
who tramples steadily on those around.

This again is my antagonist:
a pedant of minor adversarial skills
on a constant hot line to eternity
and who is blind to peoples' disregard for him.

But here is the essential shape of my antagonist:
a chronic wrangler who fears real swords,
who has withered down to a smaller size
and through whose pen the venom flows.

I must set out in search of my antagonist.
I value him more dearly than all my friends
because he is vibrantly alive,
and I carry dead flesh which will remain untried
until we pull out our knives face to face.

Ar an dTraein go Dún Éideann

(*Ar bhás Sheáin Uí Riada*)

(i)

Ar an dtraein go Dún Éideann
bhí Albanach 'nár bhfarradh,
go tóstalach faoi fhilleadh beag,
ag baothchaint gan mhairg,
laoch beag áiféiseach
a dhíon mé feadh tamaill
ar an dtonn cheoil ó Éirinn
a bhí ag caoineadh do mhairbh.

(ii)

Ní rabhas-sa ann an lá úd go raibh Cúil Aodha lán ded mharbh,
ceoltóirí ag seinm ceolta duit mar bheidís ar bhainis,
ceoltóirí ag seinm deora duit as na mílte súl carad,
ceoltóirí mar mhná caointe agat is tú id chur insan talamh.

Ní rabhas-sa ann an lá úd go raibh Cúil Aodha ar fad faoin
dtuile,
do mhuintir á dtachtadh is an tonn orthu ag briseadh —
ar an dtraein go Dún Éideann ba é an giob-geab mo thaca
is tú id bháthadh faoi do cheol féin i bpoll insan talamh.

(iii)

Ar an dtraein go Dún Éideann
bhris an tonn orm faoi dheireadh,
ar an dtraein go Dún Éideann
bhain do cheol mé dem bhonna.

(iv)

Tonn do bháis
do bhris ar chách,
ach ní dhearna díobháil bhuan
don té bhí ins na tanaíocha:
do scuab dem dhromsa

On the Express to Edinburgh

(on the death of Seán Ó Riada)

(i)

On the express to Edinburgh
a Scotsman was our companion,
ostentatious in a kilt,
blithely jabbering.
A ridiculous mould of hero,
he stemmed for a time
the wave of music from Ireland
which was keening your passing.

(ii)

I was not there the day Cúil Aodha was in frenzy,
musicians making music for you as if at your wedding,
musicians sowing tears in a thousand friends' eyes,
musicians like keening women as you were laid in your grave.

I was not there the day Cúil Aodha was deeply flooded,
your family being choked in the breaking wave of sorrow,
on the express to Edinburgh natter natter was my prop
as you were drowned by your own music in a hole in the
ground.

(iii)

On the express to Edinburgh
at last the wave broke me,
on the express to Edinburgh
your music swept through me.

(iv)

Your death-wave
shocked countless people
but for us who hug the shallows
the damage did not last —
it swept from me

d'aon bhuille amháin
mo chruit leamhais is leadráin
a ghreamaigh de ghrinneall mé,
is seolaim inniu chomh slán,
chomh haclaí, chomh folláin,
le breac ag snámh
gan cuimhneamh trísna mogallacha.
Dia leat a Sheáin.

(v)

Dia leat a Sheáin . . .
is Dia led mhuintir thar chách,
mar do bhlaiseas arís anocht
den mhúchadh lean do bhás:
chonac méireanna do mhic
ar scáileán teilifíse —
cleití creathánacha amú
i dtír fó thoinn
ag seinm do chaointe.

in one sharp swoop
the hump of boredom
and uncertainty
which kept me grounded.
And these days I sail away
securely and adroitly
as a fish slips unaware
through the meshes
God be with you, Seán.

(v)

God be with you Seán
and with your kindred above all,
for tonight I sensed again
their continuing suffocation:
I saw your son's ten fingers
on a television screen –
trembling feathers gone astray
in an underwater land –
playing a keen.

Ar Bhás Carad

Is iomaí bás gan aird a chaoineas,
daoine nárbh eol dom ach ar éigean:
ó . . . thugas m'aghaidh le falla,
is shileas deora baotha i gan fhios,
toisc barbaracht do-shéanta Dé
a bheith ag luí ar ainniseoirí is ar leanaí,
is ar ghaolta iomadúla dem chuid féinig.
Ach nuair chuala tásc do bháis-se, a chara,
níor ghoileas
ná ní mór a chailleas codladh.
Do leanas orm sa chonair dhíreach
a leag mac glórmhar na héabhlóide síos dom:
d'itheas, d'ólas, chacas,
mhuirníos sine na teilifíse,
is rinneas cumasc ar scáileán
le maighdeana gan smál na fógraíochta.
Ná tóg orm sin,
ní fhéadfainn é a thuilleadh –
an taom dóláis a scaoileadh.
Táim éirithe, a chara, as mo bhás féin a chaoineadh.

Elegy on the Death of a Friend

I can scarcely count the deaths I have lamented,
acquaintances, often, I have barely known to speak to,
and on occasion
have been forced, face to wall,
foolish and distraught,
because of God's barbarity
striking children, or guileless people.
But when I heard, dear friend, of your decease,
I didn't weep
or lose much sleep,
but kept strictly to the neat solution
mapped out in his eternal cerebrations
by the blessed son of evolution:
I ate, drank, evacuated,
fondled the television tit,
and fornicated on celluloid
with the virgins undefiled
who read the continuity bit.
Forgive me friend, I can't release
another cry of grief.
Even my own death has ceased to make me weep.

Nuair Shínfead Siar

A Chríost ná scaoil orm an bás i gan fhios
mar scaoilis orm codladh inné,
ach deonaigh dom an mhíogarnach ghnáthúil
sara gcartfaidh siad an teampall cré . . . .

Chun ná dúiseoinn, 's gur díthreabh mo dhúchas,
tír nárbh eol dom bean ná gaol,
sceach-bhall ceoigh 'nar shearg na finniúna
mhilseodh an teanga, reamhar le scéan.

Go n-atfadh romham go sleamhain insa chiúineas
an abhainn dhubh le múnlach daol,
go labharfadh chūgham an eala le muc-ghnúsacht
's an gadhar bacach le tíogar-bhéic.

Gurb iad na héin a cheolfadh dom gan suaimhneas,
ceirteacha uaigneacha le gaoth
ag liobar-chaint 's ag seint go stracaithe
ar shreanga teileafóin an aeir.

Go bhfliuchfaí mé sa cheo, is fós ná silfeadh
aon bhraon le fuarthan ar mo bhéal,
go siúlfainn is go siúlfainn i measc daoine
ag prap-ghluaiseacht mar bhréagáin ar théid . . . .

A Chríost ná scaoil orm mo chodladh i gan fhios
mar scaoilis orm bás inné,
ach deonaigh dom cnead-mhíogarnach ghnáthúil
an tseanduine i ndeireadh an lae.

Chun go leagfad fén gcathaoir mo léine chaite,
oíche shailm-chiúin, tráth Tenebrae,
is go bhfáiscfead fém chulaith suain mo chrios, le teannas,
's go sínfead siar mo theampall cré.

Before they Bundle up this House of Clay

Dear Christ don't visit me with sudden death
the way you came with sudden sleep yesterday.
Allow me please the usual time to doze
before they bundle up this house of clay.

I wouldn't wake to find my place a desert,
a land devoid of kindred, wife or child,
a foggy spot of withered vines where nothing
can ease the terror on a bloated tongue,

where in silence the smooth black river
swells up with beetles' excrement,
where a swan grunts towards me like a pig
and a lame pup outroars the tiger,

where songbirds who sing for me unceasingly
are rags of clothing mumbling on the wind,
strumming torn tunes over and over
on the desolate telephone wires,

where there is mist but no drop of water
trickling on my parched and cracked lips,
where I walk and walk in crowds
who strut like robots on a lead,

Dear Christ don't visit me with sudden sleep
as you visited me with sudden death yesterday,
allow me please the dozing time I'll need,
an old man at the butt-end of his days,

to place my tattered shirt beneath my chair
on a quiet night of psalms at Tenebrae,
to fasten the cord around my night-attire
and lay down carefully my house of clay.

II

PICTIÚIR TÍ AGUS TÍRE / INTERIORS AND EXTERIORS

Cág

Cág
ag snámhaíl gan aird
faoin spéir bhalbh;
nuair nocht fuinneog sna scamaill
d'éirigh de gheit sa ghorm,
is go hobann
do labhair le húdarás.

Uisce

Inniu
tar éis trí lá cráite
i ngátar uisce,
do líon píopaí is dabhaigh is teainceanna
go raibh ár gcluasa ag cur thar maoil
's an tigh ar crith, le binneas.
Amárach
stóinseoidh cluasa is fallaí
is dearúdfaimid an t-aoibhneas seo arís.

The Crow

The crow
flapped along
under dumb grey skies;
but finding a gap in the clouds
he shot up into the blue,
and with authority
squawked.

Water

Today,
after three bitter
waterless days,
pipes and cisterns and tanks filled
until our ears overflowed
and the house trembled with music.
Tomorrow
our ears and our walls will be sealed,
this joy lost to us again.

Díle Samhraidh

Thit díle chiúin,
do múchadh éin,
steall gach píopa
thíos is thuas,
bratacha uisce
ag sleamhain-rith
ar chéimeanna
an chosáin fúinn.
'An amhla,' arsan leanbh liom,
'nach féidir leis an uisce siúl.'

Grian Fómhair

An chearc uisce
d'imigh de sceit faoin bport,
ní dubh ná donn
ná mion a bhí sí,
ach míorúilteach mór breacórga.
Éan gréagach is ea gach éan
faoin ngrian
tráthnóna Fómhair.

Summer Rain

A sudden deluge
silenced the birds,
with the downpipes
gushing at both ends,
and a wave of water
falling over itself
on the steps
of the footpath down below.
'I suppose', the child said,
'the water cannot walk.'

Autumn Sunlight

The waterhen
startled by the river-bank
was not black, nor brown,
nor stunted,
but miraculously great and golden
Every bird has fine feathers
under the sunlight
of an afternoon in autumn.

Bó Uaigneach

An bhó dhubh aonair
ar leaca cnoic
tráthnóna geimhridh
le buíú gréine –
nuair chlaon im threo
go hingearach dearóil
's gur chuardaigh m'aghaidh,
dob iontach liom
nár thit le faill
isteach im bhachlainn.

Ceol Fómhair

Is ceol téad im chluais
na duilleoga buí fáin
ag titim gan fuaim
ar an díon dearg stáin.

Taibhreamh

Scuaidrín éan ar shreang:
anuas, de phlimp, an fogha
gan choinne,
is greamaíonn dhá ghob éin
i gcúl bog mo mhuinéil
le binb,
iad ag tolladh is ag tolladh
go mbíonn siad báite sa bhfeoil –
ach tá daoine anois á mbogadh
(is tá an fhuinneog romham ag sileadh solais)
im fhuascailt ón sceon.

Cow

The lone black cow
on the steep slope
of a winter evening
as the sun weakened –
when it leaned towards me
at an angle of misery
and plumbed my face,
it was a wonder
it didn't drop down
into my outstretched arms.

Autumn Music

I hear string music
when stray yellow leaves
fall soundlessly down
on a red tin roof.

A Dream

Birds lined up on high tension wires:
suddenly, downwards, the attack is mounted,
two bird-beaks with venom
lodge in the soft tissue of my neck
drilling drilling drilling
immersed in flesh.
But people now are putting them to flight
– and the window I see before me is pouring light –
delivering me from early morning terror.

Leac Oighir sa Chiúnas

An tráthnóna gréine seo ba chlos
mar bheadh páipéar briosc gan sos
á chorraí ar na hinsí siocaithe
cois abhann,
mar bhí uisce mánla ag cuimilt
le poirt is paistí reoite
is, sa chiúnas gorm glan,
á leá.
Ach anois 's an oíche ag titim
cloisim cnagadh obann –
tá eala ag comhrac leis an oighear.

Sollúntacht an Mhion-Éin

Seasann scuaine ealaí ar an bport
ag lúbadh a muineál tráthnóna Geimhridh –
's imíonn cearc uisce tharstu leis an sruth
i dtreo an bhaile mhóir ag snámh ar séirse,
í ag luascadh síos is suas, ag croitheadh a cinn,
's í dírithe ar chúram trom (nach léir dom).
Ach ní suim leis na healaí mion-éan sollúnta duairc:
leanaid orthu ag lúbadh a muineál sa bhfuacht
go díomhaoin maorga.

Ice Quietly

All through the sunlit afternoon
was a sound like crisp tissue
crackling on the frozen wetlands
by the water's edge,
as the river stroked gently
along iced up banks and frozen patches
in the clean blue silence,
hastening the thaw.
But now, at nightfall,
I hear the rough beating
– a swan thrashing at the ice.

The Solemnity of a Minor Bird

On a winter's afternoon a line of swans
stand on a riverbank uncoiling their white necks,
A waterhen goes briskly by, swimming
with the current, making towards the town;
it jockeys up and down with bobbing head
bent solemnly on some errand (of God knows whose
devising).
But the swans pay no attention to a solemn minor bird;
they continue in the chilly air looping their white necks
majestical and idle.

Múscailt Bhréige

Mothú earraigh,
lá maoth;
spéir ghorm nite,
síonaíl éan;
madra ag tafann
mar bheadh i gcarcar
domhain faoi thalamh
in imigéin;
uisce ag sileadh
go scímghlórach
trí fhallaí cloch
ar bhlaincéadaí
úrghlasa an bhóthair . . . .

Is na crainn mhóra
seasann siad
lom is righin
is sochraidiúil
ar chúl gach claí,
ag súil le sú
nach bhfuil le fáil.

Múscailt bhréige,
peata lae
gan líonrith
gan fás.

A False Awakening

A sense of spring,
a soft day,
small birds chirp
under a washed blue sky,
a dog barks
from some dungeon
deep in earth,
remote in space,
water runs
with swishing sounds
through stone walls
onto the green blankets
of the road . . . .

But the mammoth trees
behind each wall and ditch
stand still –
funereal and bare,
recalcitrant –
expecting sap
that fails to rise,

A false spring,
a pet day,
no growth at all,
no ecstasy.

III

AIDHE! / AYE!

(From a Greek Diary / Dréachtaí Dialainne, 1977-80)

Do Stoitheas Luibh

Do stoitheas luibh
ar an gconair gharbh,
is seal ina dhiaidh sin
nuair a leagas méar liom
ar mo leacain,
d'imigh cumhracht *eucalyptus*
ina sconna aoibhnis
trí mo shrón go dtí mo dhrólann.
Tuigeadh dom ansin
go rabhas sa Ghréig.

Seilbh Tí, 1977

Fuaireamar seilbh ar thigh aréir, tigh scóipiúil aoldaite ar leaca gharbh cnoic os cionn trá iargúlta in oileán sa Ghréig. Níl radharc ar thigh eile ná ar dhaoine in aon ghiorracht dúinn. D'éiríomar ar maidin ar a hocht is do ritheamar corpnocht faoin ngréin isteach san bhfarraige. Comhlíonadh aislinge ab ea an méid sin: aisling a ghin scannáin Hollywood ionam as m'óige i dtaobh an iompair is dual don duine i bParthas saolta. . . . Bhí nathair nimhe inár bhfarradh, ámh, nár samhlaíodh riamh sna scannáin: smugairle róin bídeach a chuir cealg ghránna ionam an túisce thomas san uisce. B'éigean dom mé féin a leigheas ar an modh Gréagach: mo mhún féin a chuimilt den chréacht. Ina dhiaidh sin do shocraíomar síos i bParthas.

I Picked a Herb

I picked a herb
on the rough track,
and straightaway
brushing a finger
across my cheek
the scent of eucalyptus
poured joyfully into
the core of my being.
And then I knew
I'd arrived in Greece.

Moving In, 1977

We moved in last night, into a spacious whitewashed house on a rough hillside overlooking a deserted strand on a Greek Island. There's no other house in sight, and nobody near us. At eight this morning we got up and ran to the sea naked under the sun. All that was a fulfilment of a vision; a vision born out of Hollywood pictures when I was a boy, telling me how to behave when in an earthly paradise. . . . A snake was discerned in our midst, however, of a kind you would not expect in a film: a tiny jellyfish that stung me horribly as soon as I plunged into the water. I used the Greeks' own remedy for it, and rubbed my own piss into the wound. And only then did we settle into Eden.

An t-Arán Laethúil

Saol srianta na mainistreach atá á chaitheamh anseo againn: tráta, blúire cáise, canta aráin, caora fíniúna, is gloine *retsina* am lóin; blúire feola is sailéad sa *taverna* istoíche (nuair a bhímid sásta an naoi míle fada achrannach de bhóthar a chur dínn, ann is ar ais). Idir dhá linn, snámh, scríbhneoireacht, léitheoireacht agus scíth. Gach ní rialta. Titeann an oíche an-obann. Anocht chonaiceamar an ghrian ag dul faoi ina meall mór cruinn dearg ar ghob tíre i bhfad amach san bhfarraige. Plab! d'imigh a leath i bhfarraige. Plab eile, agus bhí sí imithe as radharc ar fad. D'fhan dathanna do-inste — ó dhearg go corcra, is ó ghlas go dúghorm — ar an uisce go ceann i bhfad. Níos déanaí ar an mbalcóin chonaiceamar uainn faoin spéir ard réiltíneach na soilse ar mhórthír na Gréige, agus soilse na dteaincéirí móra a bhíonn ag déanamh a slí (a deirtear liom) ó Istanbul go dtí Murascaill na Peirse. Ní raibh glór duine ná asail ná madra le cloisint, ach fo-ghlaoch ón gceann cait sna cnoic. Nuair a shiúlamar ar an trá faoi sholas na gealaí bhí cáithníní solais ag léimt aníos chugainn ón gcúr ar bharr na toinne.

Daily Bread

Here we live a life of simple monastic order: a tomato, a hunk of cheese, a lump of bread, grapes, and a glass of retsina at mid-day; a slice of meat with salad in the taverna at night (provided we're willing to walk the nine long miles over the rough road, there and back). Apart from that there's swimming, writing, reading and taking things easy. All in order. Night falls without warning. This evening we watched the sun setting as a great round red mass on a headland jutting well out into the sea. Flop! It was half gone under the surface. Flop again, and it disappeared from sight altogether. Wonderful colours – from red to purple, from green to dark-blue – lingered on the water for a long time after. Later, from the balcony, we saw the lights from the Greek mainland under a high and starry sky, and the lights of the big tankers sailing (so I'm told) from Istanbul to the Persian Gulf. There was not a living sound to be heard, not a man nor a donkey nor a dog, except for an occasional cry from the owl on the hillside. As we walked the beach in the moonlight there were flecks of light jumping up at us from the foam on the breaking waves.

Ella!

Lá mór brothaill. Ní minic a chuireann aon duine an chonair gharbh de go dtí an trá againne. Déanach ar maidin, ámh, tháinig beirt de bhuachaillí óga ar rothar gluaiste agus fuadach nimhe fúthu. B'éigean dóibh an rothar a chaitheamh uathu tamall suas ar leaca an chnoic, ansin rith siad le fána ar buile, agus do stoith siad díobh na léinteacha. 'Ella!' do liúigh duine acu agus é ag léimt isteach sa taoide.

Ar Ghrinneall Abhann

Chuamar ag siúl inné ar ghrinneall tirim na habhann idir F. agus an trá. Bhí toir ghlasa ar gach taobh dínn, tuigí caola fada den bhambú, is garbhchlocha tuathalacha go tiubh faoinár mbonna. Feadh na slí ní raibh de chuideachta againn go ceann i bhfad ach féileacáin bhána ag sníomh rompu tríd an aer, is éiníní beaga bídeacha (nár aithníos) ag gearrléimnigh ar na poirt. Gan choinne timpeall ar chúinne do nocht chugainn Gréagach mná: í leathan álainn, í dúdhonn ina craiceann, sciorta ornáideach breac uirthi, siogairlíní ina cluasa, seáilín cinn dathannach uirthi mar a bheadh ar ghiofóg. Ghabh sí tharainn mar a bheadh sí ar bhóthar an rí, agus bhí a súile donna ag preabarnaigh ina ceann.

Ella!

A long sweltering day. Hardly anyone ever takes the rough track leading to our beach. In the late morning, however, two young fellows with motor bikes turned up full of fire and frenzy. They had to abandon their bikes on the slope, and then they ran wild and free, throwing off their clothes. 'Ella!' hallooed one of them, as he plunged into the waves.

On the River Bed

Yesterday we walked along the dried-up bed of the river between F. and the beach. There were green bushes to each side of us, tall thin shoots of bamboo, and large awkward stones strewn everywhere beneath our feet. During much of our walk we were alone except for white butterflies threading the air, and tiny little birds (I don't know the name) hopping on the banks. Suddenly a Greek woman appeared around a bend; she was broad and beautiful, with a swarthy skin, wearing a patterned speckled skirt, pendants in her ears, a bright head-shawl like a gipsy. To us she looked as if she was walking the king's highway, with her brown eyes dancing in her head.

Sagart Gréagach

Bhí cuireadh dinnéir againn le déanaí go dtí tigh C. An bóthar ard a ghabhann thar a áit chónaithe, tá sé ar aon chothrom le díon an tí aige. Bhíomar ag ithe linn go scléipeach sa chlós thíos faoi aer cumhra na hoíche, na lampaí lasta, fíon ar bord, nuair a sheas an sagart go hobann ar dhíon an tí os ár gcionn, mar a bheadh préachán ollmhór coimhthíoch: róbaí fada dubha air, bairéad cruinn dubh, féasóg thiubh liath, agus cuachóg ar a ghruaig thiar. Fad a bhí sé ag labhairt linn bhí a lámha leata aige sa chlapsholas is a mhuinchillí scuabacha ag gabháil na gaoithe. Fáidh a déarfá, a thuirling ón domhan uachtarach agus soiscéal iontais aige le craoladh? Nuair a tuigeadh a chaint is a iompar ba léir, áfach, nach raibh uaidh ach bia agus deoch. Boladh an rósta agus na scléipe a thug an braineán an-aithnid seo ón Eaglais Ghréagach ar dhíon tí os ár gcionn.

Ceann Cait

Oícheanta bána maothghealaí. Aréir agus sinn inár gcodladh faoin spéir laistiar den tigh do nocht an ghealach mhór os cionn an fhalla cúil is do stán orainn mar a dhéanfadh bráthair bocht mothaolach. Ní raibh d'fhuaim le cloisint ach na crainn *eucalyptus* is na crainn ológa ag siosarnaigh go ciúin sa ghaoth. Ansin is ea do labhair an ceann cait faoi mar a bheadh sé tuirlingte ar an bhfalla os ár gcomhair, go mall soiléir caithréimeach ceolmhar — í-á-úc — is do bhain an anáil dínn. Ní scréach a dhéanann an ceann cait Gréagach seo ach ceol fliúite.

The Greek Priest

A little time ago we were invited to dinner at C's house. The road by his house is on a level with the roof. We were outside eating merrily in the yard in the night-scented air, lamps glowing, wine going around, when suddenly above us was the priest standing on the roof of the house, like a huge alien crow, with his long black soutane, his round black biretta, his thick grey beard, and his hair tied back in a knot. While he talked to us his hands were spread out in the twilight and the sweep of his sleeves caught the breeze. An apparition come down from the world beyond with a wondrous message to tell, perhaps? Not so, alas. When his message and his behaviour were understood, it was clear that all he wanted was a sup to drink and a bite to eat. The smell of roast meat, and the noise of festivity, had brought this unknown scald-crow from the Greek Church on to the rooftop above us.

Owl

Soft pale moonlit nights. Last night while we slept outside behind the house the moon showed itself above the back wall and stared in at us like a poor guileless lay-brother. The only sound to be heard was the eucalyptus trees and the olive trees shuffling quietly in the night air. Then the owl sounded as if it had just perched on the wall across from us, slow and clear and confident and sonorous – ee-aw-ook – and took our breath away. Owls do not hoot or screech in Greece, they make flute music.

Claisceadal na nAsal

Braithimid uainn na hasail anseo . . . agus crónú mall na hoíche. Nuair a bhíomar i dtigh eile ar an oileán seo tamall, bhíodh radharc difriúil ar fad againn le titim oíche. Le claonú gréine do chorcraíodh an solas ar na cnoic agus d'éiríodh an talamh crón, dúchrón, breac-chrón: na sceacha glasdonna briogadánacha, an coinleach garbh órbhuí, na bolláin charraige — iad uile ag crónú leo, is ag druidim chugat isteach an doras, ba dhóigh leat, le muintearas.

B'in é an t-am go dtéadh na hasail thar bráid, na cloig ag clingeadh ar a muineál, glórtha daoine agus ceol á dtionlacan sa chlapsholas crón. Líon tí a bheadh ann go minic ag déanamh ar an mbaile mór: fear ag marcaíocht, b'fhéidir, ar an asal, a bhean agus a chuid leanaí ag siúl ina dhiaidh go cainteach, *transistor* ag buachaill óg acu agus ceol Theodorakis ag pléascadh as ar fud an gcnoc. Uaireanta eile is ag iompar earraí le haghaidh a ndíolta ar an mbaile a bheadh an t-asal. Oíche amháin chuala asal ag méiligh, mheasas, nuair a dhéanadh an marcach é bhrostú chun siúil. Nuair a fhéachas níos cruinne chonac cloigeann mionnáin ag gobadh aníos go scanraithe as gach ceann den dá mhála a bhí ar shrathar an asail.

Níos déanaí, nuair a cheanglaítí iad sna goirt le haghaidh na hoíche, is ea chuireadh na hasail iad féin in iúl i gceart: gol, olagón, is búir-theach fholamh uaigneach. Bhíodh roinnt acu a mbíodh sreangáin a ngutha ag crith is ag caoineadh tamall sula bhféadfaidís aon ghlór ceart a dhéanamh. Roinnt eile acu ag déanamh glóir mar a bheadh adharc is ag baint macalla as na cnoic mór-thimpeall. Is do chaithidís tamall den oíche mar sin ag freagairt a chéile ó ghort go gort, is ó ghleann go gleann. Iad i bpéin gnéis, is dócha.

Donkey Concert

We miss the donkeys here . . . and the slow yellow-brown twilights. When we had another house on this island a while back, our view was altogether different at nightfall. As the sun dipped, the light turned purple on the hills, and the earth became yellow-brown, speckled brown, dark brown. The prickly green-brown bushes, the rough golden stubble, the boulders – all would seem to become browner and closer, finally pushing in a friendly fashion right into our room.

Around that time the donkeys would pass by, bells clinking at their necks, the sounds of people and music accompanying them in the fading twilight. You'd often see a complete household on the road to the town: the man astride the donkey, as likely as not, with his wife and children walking behind and chatting, one of the young fellows carrying a transistor blasting the music of Theodorakis over the hills. At other times the donkey would be loaded with produce for sale in the town. One night I seemed to hear a donkey bleating when his rider forced him to go faster. When I looked more closely I could see the head of a terrified kid goat sticking up out of each of the two sacks slung across the donkey's straddle.

Later, when they were tethered in the field overnight, the donkeys let themselves go properly; crying, keening and howling in a desolate empty way. The vocal chords of some of them would shiver and whinge for a while before they could make any proper noise. Others could sound off like a bugle striking an echo from the hills all around. And so they spent some of the night like that, calling to each other from field to field, and from valley to valley. They were suffering, I suppose, from sex-starvation.

Ógbhean Ghréagach

Tá ógbhean aonair foltdhubh san uisce ar an trá gainimhe faoi bhun ár dtí. Tá an t-aigéan gléineach timpeall uirthi ag glioscarnaigh. Seasann sí neomat beag gan cor, is chím go bhfuil a cíocha nochta. Ansin cuimlíonn sí siar a duala dubha, cuireann a dhá láimh faoi chúl a cinn is síneann ar a droim san uisce gormghlas go síodúil macnasach faoi theas na gréine. Aidhe!

Múchadh na Gréine

Maidin inniu líon scamaill éadroma isteach os cionn na trá againn — scamaill bheaga bhána, scamaill chaola liatha. Níos déanaí nuair a bhíos ag gabháil an bóthar garbh os cionn an chnoic i radharc trá F. (trá na dturasóirí) do múchadh an ghrian orm de gheit, is thuirling duairceas. Chonac uaim sa drochsholas daoine fásta, a leanaí, a madraí, ar bholg na trá, agus ba dhóigh liom nár tharraing aon chréatúr acu a anáil le halltacht go ceann neomat mór amháin. *Lèse majesté* is ea an ghrian a mhúchadh ina séasúr féin sa Ghréig. . . .

D'fhoighnigh formhór na gcuairteoirí go gruama ar an trá — iad chomh brúite le hucht saoire cois na farraige in Éirinn. I gceann tamaill thit dornán de bhraonacha ramhra fearthainne, ach — murab ionann is in Éirinn — thosaigh an glanadh gorm gan mhoill arís.

The Greek Girl

There's a solitary blackhaired girl in the water on the strand beneath our house. The shining seas glisten around her. She stands for a moment unmoving and I see that her breasts are bare. Then she smooths back her dark hair, puts her hands behind her head and lies back into the blue-green water, lapped and fondled under the sun's warmth. Aye!

The Sun Put Out

This morning the bay in front of us filled with thin clouds – small white clouds, wispy grey clouds. Later as I made my way up the rough track across the hill in sight of the beach at F. (the tourists' beach) the sun suddenly disappeared, and gloom descended. Below me in the half-light I saw grown-ups, their children, their dogs, in the middle of the beach, and it looked to me as if not one of them so much as drew breath for a long moment. To put out the sun during its appointed time in Greece is *lèse-majesté*, nothing less.

Most of the visitors just stood around gloomily on the beach – as depressed as holidaymakers at the seaside in Ireland. After a while a few heavy drops of rain fell, but then – unlike in Ireland – the skies began clearing to blue again.

Seanbhean Ghréagach

Tá formhór na dturasóirí imithe agus *meltheme* crua ag séideadh. Beidh Kyrie Irene ag fágaint a botháin samhraidh cois na trá i F. gan aon mhoill is ag filleadh ar an seantigh ar an gcnoc. Ag buachailleacht mionnán gabhair a chaitheann sí a saol anseo: iad mar a bheadh eilití óga — dubh, bán, rua, breac — siar is aniar de sciúirdeanna reatha sa choinleach donn scáinte ar aghaidh an tí aici.

Chonac uaim í ar an trá fholamh i F. ó chianaibh, a haghaidh seirgthe rocach, í faoina gúna fada ciardhubh agus faoina seáilín cinn atá chomh dubh céanna. Thrusáil sí na muinchillí, d'ardaigh a gúna is thosaigh ar a cosa caola bána a ní sa sáile. Beidh sí chomh hoiriúnach le haon duine dínne, na cuairteoirí donna deasa, le haghaidh an gheimhridh!

Turasóirí, 1980

Tá na turasóirí ag dul i líonmhaire anseo in aghaidh na bliana. Inniu sheoil *caique* dathannach lán de Shasanaigh isteach an trá chugainn, agus bhí ceol *transistors* ag réabadh na spéire againn go ceann na n-uaireanta fada. Do nocht roinnt de na turasóirí, idir fhir agus mhná, iad féin go craiceann. Chuadar ag snámh, bhí picnic acu, d'fhágadar dramhaíl ina ndiaidh ar fud na trá. St. Tropez eile a bheidh anseo nuair a fheabhsóidh na bóithre. Cheana féin tá bóthar garbh déanta thar an droim isteach chugainn: agus tá conair de shaghas éigin á gearradh ar an droim amach uainn, chomh maith. Chuamar ag siúl ar an droim sin cúpla lá ó shin, tríd an *maquis* garbh briogadánach atá lán de luibheanna cumhra. Bhí an maide siúil agam ag fágaint boladh na tíme brúite ina dhiaidh. Níl aon áitreabh ar an droim seo, ach chonaiceamar cúpla póna caorach, roinnt seanláithreán buailte, agus fo-thigh tite a bhí stóinsithe tráth. Bhí daoine anseo anallód, daoine a dhein gáire agus gol agus mioscais, daoine ar nós Danny Garvey agus Jimmy Mhártain i nDún Chaoin — agus gan ann anois ach turasóirí. Níor thaitin sé liom nach raibh ionam féin ach turasóir

Old Greek Woman

Nearly all the tourists have left and the bitter *meltheme* is blowing. Soon Kyrie Irene will move out of her summer hut next to the strand in F. and go back to the old house up the hill. She spends her life herding goat kids; they are like young deer — black, white, brown, piebald — as they dart hither and thither across the thin tawny stubble in front of her house.

A while back I saw her in the distance on the deserted beach in F., her face weatherbeaten and wrinkled, wearing a coal-black dress and a headshawl just as black. She rolled up the sleeves, lifted her dress, and set to washing her thin pale legs in the sea. She will be as ready as any one of us, as any smoothly tanned tourist, for the coming winter.

Tourists, 1980

Each year more and more tourists find their way here. Today a brightly coloured caique full of Brits dropped anchor off our beach, and the air was rent with loud transistors for hours. Some of the trippers, both men and women, stripped to the buff. They swam, they picnicked, they left their mark, and their refuse, all over the beach. It will turn into another St Tropez here once the roads are improved. There's already a rough road leading here over the hill behind us: and there's a passage being cut through the next hill, as well. We went walking there a couple of days ago, through the wild scrubby maquis full of scented herbs. The stick I carried left a smell of crushed thyme after it. There is no dwelling on this hill, but we saw a couple of sheep pounds, old cattle shelters, and ruined out-houses that had once stood ruggedly. People lived here long ago, people who laughed and wept and hated, people who were like Danny Garvey and Jimmy Mhártain in Dún Chaoin — and now only tourists come. I didn't relish the

chomh maith leo: nach raibh aon eolas dá laghad agam ar an muintir seo go rabhas ag siúl ar fhothracha a dtithe, ar a láithreáin bhuailte, ar a gcnámha.

Nuair a bhaineamar na faillteacha arda amach ar an taobh thall de chnoc, agus ár gcosa scólta, do ghlaoigh na héin mhara faoi sceon gur ritheadar as anáil.

Chuimhníos nár chuala éan mara ag gíogalaigh cois trá againn féin i mbliana. Bliain éigin acu seo nuair a chuirfear tarra ar na bóithre, ní chloisfear iad ar na faillteacha anseo ach oiread. Teitheann na héin mhara féin roimh thurasóirí. Ní fada, is dócha, go leanfaimid féin na héin. . . .

thought that I myself was only there as a tourist as much as any of them; that I knew absolutely nothing about the people whose ruined houses I walked on, their threshing floors, their bones.

When we got to the high cliffs on the far side of the hill, our legs scalded, the sea-birds were crying out wildly with their might and main.

I recalled that this year I had not heard the sea-birds crying on the side where our strand was. One of these years when the roads are tarred, neither will they be heard on the cliffs here. Even the sea-birds give way to the tourists. Before long, no doubt, we ourselves will follow the birds. . . .

IV

TURASÓIR SA GHRÉIG/ A TOURIST IN GREECE

Síos Linn

Seo sinn ar deireadh
in uisce na Gréige,
na púiríní daite
ar an imeall ár mbréagadh,
crios fuar faoinár gcom
d'uisce glas gléineach,
's ár dtroithe ar grinneall
ag glinniúint faoin ngréin seo.
Léim síos is suas liom,
amach thar ár n-airde,
tarraingeoidh mé síos tú
is tiocfaidh tú aníos chūgham,
síos linn le chéile
faoi theas is faoi phléisiúr,
síos linn le chéile
is múchfar araon sinn . . . .

Sin deireadh ar deireadh
le laethanta liatha.

Siúlóid sa Chréit

Do shiúlamar ar chosán cré an chnoic
faoi scáth na gcrann, fionnuar sa teas,
oráistí, tite, ag lonradh ins na díoga,
táipéis d'ológa dú faoi bhun ár gcos.
Ar chasadh dúinn abhaile le luí gréine
do dheargaigh, le cúirtéis, an chonair romhainn,
is nuair labhair an ceann cait chūghainn ón maoileann
dúraís-se 'mairfimíd anois go deo.'

Greek Waters

Here at the end
we've come to Greek waters,
beachpebbles, all colours,
from fairy-book stories;
our waists feel the girdle
of lucid green ocean,
our feet at seabottom
are glinting in sunlight.
Let's jump up and down,
move out of our depth,
I'll bring you down with me,
you'll surface back to me,
let's plunge down together –
to full suffocation.

Let's put an end here
to the grey days of Ireland.

A Walk in Crete

We walked the earthen mountain trail
shaded by trees from scorching sun,
fallen oranges glowed in ditches,
a tapestry of olives underfoot.
Returning home under a lavish sunset
our path flushed red in courtesy,
and when an owl spoke from a summit
you said 'we'll live forever now'.

Ar Bhóthar Cnoic sa Chréit

Ar bhóthar cnoic sa Chréit
chuaigh baintreach álainn tharainn,
baintreach óg na gruaige doinne
is bláithfhleasc in a baclainn,
sochraid ban in éadaí dú
ina diaidh aniar á leanúint,
iad ag triall roimh dheireadh lae
d'fhonn deasghnátha caointe a fhearadh.

Taréis tamaill d'éirigh chūghainn
boladh mealltach cumhra ón reilig,
boladh túise á dó faoin ngréin,
ár ngriogadh is ár dtachtadh,
is d'airíomar an bás ag snámh
go milis mall faoin spéir mhór ghorm.

Cumar ins an Chréit

Tá fhios agamsa cumar ins an Chréit
ag cur thar maoil le horáistí fiáine,
crainn chaince, tím, liomóidí is mismín
's na scórtha eile luibh is fiaile.
Bíonn musc na bhflaitheas ann gach Fómhar dá
  dtagann,
duilliúr is cnuas ar gach seanchrann féin —
an té chumhrófaí ins an chumar seo
níor chreite go lobhfadh a chorp i gcré.

A Mountain Road in Crete

On a mountain road in Crete
a handsome widow passed us,
a youthful brownhaired woman
carrying a wreath of flowers;
blackgarbed women followed
in a funeral procession,
intent before the sun would set
on rites of lamentation.

Soon after in the burning sun
from the village graveyard
a seductive smell of incense rose
tantalising choking,
and we felt death crawl sweetly slowly
in the great blue sky above us.

A Ravine in Crete

I know a deep ravine in Crete
overflowing with wild oranges,
quince trees, thyme, lemons, mints,
and all sorts of other aromatic herbs and weeds;
a heavenly musk fills autumn days,
fruit and foliage on old trees and on young.
In the fragrance of this deep ravine
one can't believe the body rots in earth.

Comharthaí Aimsire

Anuraidh ar oileán sa Ghréig,
faoi ghleithearán teasa is cuileanna,
bhí caora mharbh ag bréanadh an bhealaigh
chun na trá ba rogha linn riamh:
í pollta ag míolta, lán de ghearba,
a lomra smeartha ag fuil is cré,
ag fógairt orainn nach lobhadh go brothall —
gur baol an Samhradh in Éirinn féin.

'Besides, who knows before the end what light may shine'

(in memoriam *Daniel Corkery, Seán Ó Riada,*
Seán Ó Ríordáin, Séamas Murphy)

Maidin ghorm ins an Ghréig
(an leathchéad scoite agam)
faoi bhíomaí buí is giolcaigh fhite —
mo chorp ar teitheadh ón ngréin.

Liszt go glinn im chluais ag cumasc
le lapaíl shámh na dtonn,
táim síoraí anseo sa bhfuarthan
idir fallaí bána an tí.

An túisce stopann an pianó
tránn an mhuir fém chroí,
is cuimhním ar dhaoine age baile
a bhí mór im chathair tráth.

Heat and Decay

A year ago on a small Greek island
a dead sheep in a haze of heat and flies
stenched up the path we always took
to our favourite sandy cove:
its flesh was furrowed by maggots,
the wool smeared by blood and clay;
we began to fear the hot Greek summer –
even summer in Ireland we shall fear quite soon.

'Besides, who knows before the end what light may shine'

(in memoriam *Daniel Corkery, Seán Ó Riada, Seán Ó Ríordáin, Séamas Murphy*)

A blue mid-morning here in Greece
(my fiftieth year passed by),
under mottled beams and woven reeds –
body flees from sun.

Liszt, lucid in my ears, is merging
with the soft lap of the waves,
I'm immortal in this coolness,
enclosed between white walls.

As soon as the piano ceases
the sea ebbs from my heart
and I think of people home in my city
who, not long ago, stood high.

Ceathrar fear im chathairse
a éiríonn romham sa tost,
an luisne ard do mhúscail siad
do dheineas cuimilt léi:

an saoi a chrith le gile an tsolais
i gceartain seanfhilí,
an draoi scaoil caisí ceoil thar cora —
is a bháigh é féin sa tsruth;

an file cráite a mhúnlaigh nua —
scamhóga Gaeilge dúinn,
an dealbhadóir chuir clocha ag rince
lena sheanchaíocht.

File, ceoltóir, dealbhadóir,
is rompu an máistir-saoi,
ina measc siúd do tharlaíos-sa;
ní tharlóidh sé arís.

Maidin ghorm ins an Ghréig
(an leathchéad scoite agam),
ag cuimhneamh ar an luisne a bhí,
sin é an namhaid anois.

Anois an t-am don rince aonair
ar ghainimh bheo na trá —
na cosa a chaitheamh go háiféiseach
is leá d'aonghnó sa teas.

Four men from my native city
rise before me now,
the glow of mind which they created
I rubbed against a while:

a sage who trembled at the brightness
in the forge of ancient poets,
a druid who released our dammed-up music
and perished in the flood,

a tortured poet who fashioned for us
new Irish-language lungs,
a sculptor who set headstones dancing
with his carefree lore.

Musician, poet and sculptor,
and before them master-sage,
I happened to occur amongst them,
it will not occur again.

A blue mid-morning here in Greece
(my fiftieth year passed by)
thinking of the glow that was —
that's matter for the dying.

Better rise up now, a solo-dancer,
on the hot sands of the beach,
throw out both legs absurdly,
and melt down in the sun.

Anocht sa Ghréig Cuimhním mar Chímís chūghainn ar dTúis an Solas Tóirse

Do thóg a céile rómánsúil meánaosta cúirt aoldaite di sa Ghréig
ar leacain sceirdiúil cnoic, os cionn trá báine, scoite amach ón saol.
Chuir bíomaí buí is tuigí fite dlúth faoi scáth an díona
de réir an tseana-ghnáis a chleacht na ceardaithe sa taobh sin tíre.
Bhíodar beirt ag teitheadh i bhfad i gcéin ó chultúr bréige an iarthair.

Dhein rónta i mbeagán ama dá gcuid leanaí beaga donna.
B'í féin bainríon na gcríocha ciana is siúr na gréine gile.
Le titim oíche ar an *bpatio* róst sí an gabhar don dúiche fairsing,
í féin is mná na háite ar meisce ag suainseán is ag gáirí geala.
Is dhein rincí Gréagacha ar an dtrá go maidin leis na feara.

Do scaradar go hobann 's phós sé siúd le flosc an cúigiú huair.
Dhein sise a cónaí i Los Angeles le hógfhear gorm teaspúil,
's ní cheanglódh go deo arís, adúirt, le fireannach ar mhalairt datha —
anois a thuig sí an spraoi a bhain le bheith de shíor ar bhainis.
Ach trína caint do bhraitheas cumha na Gréige ag comhrac lena gaisce. . . .

Anocht sa Ghréig cuimhním mar chímís chūghainn ar dtúis an solas tóirse,
a cúirt aoldaite fágtha aici chun braon *retsina* ól 'nár dteannta,
go nochtfaí í caol ard, docheansaithe, ar chosán garbh faille,
a gúna sleamhain dubh 's a fáinní óir ag glioscarnaigh fén ngealaigh.
Dob fhéidir leat a rá go raibh a triall, i gcónaí riamh, ar bhainis.

I Recall Tonight in Greece

Her besotted husband built a white-washed house in Greece
on a rough hill sloping sharply to a lonely beach,
with yellow beams and woven reeds snug beneath the roof
as was the style of builders in that spot.
Both were refugees (they said) from a decaying western culture.

In a wink, their brown children turned into seals,
and she became a queen and a sister of the sun.
At nightfall on her patio she roasted kid for all
and heady from the gossip and gaiety of women
danced until daylight on the beach with local men.

They split, and airily he moved on to his fifth wife.
She found herself a young and randy black in LA,
and said she never could go back to whitemen
after the rapture of this unending wedding.
But I heard the loss of Greece behind her talk.

I recall tonight in Greece the first glimpse of her torch
as she left her white-washed court to join us in a drink;
slender, tall, indomitable, she would step from the rough path,
her long black dress and rings bathed in moonlight.
In truth, she journeyed always in nuptial readiness.

Tigh sa Ghréig

Tá's agamsa seanathigh eastáit sa Ghréig,
dronuilleogach, sámh, ar thaobh na fothana,
an díon ag lúbadh faoi, graffiti ar an mbinn,
cac gabhair ar fud na cistineach.
Do shíleas tráth gurb ann a gheobhainn buanadas.

Faoi bhun a fhallaí cosanta, ar thrá bheag bhán,
do phiocamar faoin dteas púiríní leanbaí,
do shíneamar go séimh ar shíoda an aigéin
's le smugaí róin do nascas-sa mo chumann beag.
Is do thaibhríos ar mo sheanathigh athchóirithe.

Bheadh na clocha breaca faoi mhoirtéal arís,
lampaí in almóirí seomraí leapan ann,
figí á dtriomú ar dhíon neartaithe an tí
is dinnéar beirte faoin gcrann síprise ar an bpatio.
Bheadh an tigh againn chomh snoite slán le Gallaras.

Sa tobar ársa faoi na crainn ológa thíos
bheadh inneall leictreach comhachtach ciúin ag monabhar,
ag seoladh uisce leis go binn ar fud an tí
ag riar ar thrátaí, toir fíniúna, is aubergines —
réim bia ba gheal le díthreabhach nua-aimseartha.

Is chuirfinn coite beag sa tsnámh i ndeireadh lae
go dtí an baile poirt aolnite trasna uainn
(mara gcloistear cloig thráthrialta neamhurchóideacha
ag clingireacht faoi ghormdhíon an teampaill ann),
is faoi thuairim ár dtí nua d'ólfaimis go maidin ann.

Ach sara mbainfimis ár nead amach arís
chuardóimis na cúinní i nuachtáin Shasana
ag súil le scéal thar drompla díleann chūghainn aniar —
cé bhuaigh Craobh na hÉireann, ar thit an Rialtas fós,
nó an raibh laghdú ar an gcáin ioncaim ar deireadh thiar?

A House in Greece

I know a lodge on an old estate in Greece,
cosy rectangular shaded from the wind,
the roof sagging sadly, graffiti on the walls,
goats' excrement strewed around the living room.
I thought one time I'd stake there my claim for permanence.

Under the defensive walls on a small white strand
in raging heat we picked fine pebble stones,
we stretched out softly on the ocean's silk
and I began to lose my hate of jellyfish.
And kept on imagining my Grecian home's refurbishment.

The variegated stone we'd have pointed once again,
oil-lamps would light up niches in the bedrooms there,
figs would dry securely on the newly strengthened roof
and we'd lunch *à deux* beneath the cypress on the patio.
Our house would look as smart and well-designed as Gallarus.

Beneath the olives in an ancient well
a powerful softly murmuring pump would operate,
sending water sweetly to all areas of the house,
irrigating vines, tomatoes, aubergines –
a diet to suit a modern Irish anchorite.

At day's ending we would launch our skiff
and visit the whitewashed port across from us
(where from a bluedomed temple on the hill
bells ring, innocent and punctual)
and we would toast till morning our Greek property.

But before returning to our new Greek nest
we would scour the corners of English newspapers,
hoping news would reach across the ocean deep –
who won the hurling final? did the government resign?
was there a reduction in the rate of income tax?

Mar gidh gnáth a foirne fraochda in Éirinn bhocht –
snigí caca is búir bhéal-láidre ann go follasach –
is é a scéal siúd snáithe leanúnach mo shaoil
is ní chothódh grian na Gréige mé dá uireasa . . . .

Is diaidh ar ndiaidh ar thrá sa Ghréig do tuigeadh dom
gur tar éis luí na gréine, am an tseanchais,
a leáfadh orm mo sheanathigh athchóirithe.

For though my people in the emerald isle can be unruly
– loud-mouthed boors and shit-nits flourishing –
their story has been threaded through my life-concerns
– exiled from that no Greek sun could nourish me.

So on a beach in Greece I slowly grasped
that when the sun goes down (that classic time for
  storytelling)
my refurbished Grecian home would melt – each night –
  inexorably.

V

BAOITHÍN A D'FHILL AR ÉIRINN (1956): DRÉACHT AS / BAOITHÍN RETURNS TO IRELAND (1956): AN EXTRACT

In this long poem, Baoithín, a monk in the service of Colmcille in Iona, returns to Ireland to find his people in torpor, capable of little activity beyond that of erecting statues to the illustrious dead. This extract deals with Baoithín's visit to his own relatives in an Irish-speaking district.

(i)

Ar mhair go fóill dem ghaolta, an file is an t-iascaire,
do chanadar d'aonghuth: 'Seo é an talamh
méith, an tír 'nar éag na máithreacha 's gur seoladh
uainn na gearrchailí i gcéin, an tír nár fhan aon
fhosaíocht ag na hasail 's go mairimíd ar dhéirc
ón spéir; an tír ná facathas le cuimhne daoine
aon tsúgradh leanbh, ná radharc ar bhád á iompar chun
na mara, ná maidrín ar éill ag port feadaíle
ag filleadh abhaile tar éis lae fiaigh. Seo é an talamh
méith: mar tuigtear dúinn gan bhréig, ó chainteanna
a thagann chūghainn ar aer isteach, gurb anso
tá faoileán bán na beatha nách dán dár muintir teacht
i dtír á cheal; 's gur sinne, an file is an t-iascaire,
is a maireann farainn fós de bhráithre
aontumha na mbróga briste, is cosantóirí geanmnaí
ar bheo éanúil na seansibhialtachta,
's dá bharr go mbeifear fós ár moladh i bhfad i ndiaidh
ár mbáis. ('S dá bharr, go dtógfar dealbh dúinn go hard
i dtearmann seo an fhaoileáin bháin.)'

(ii)

'Féach i leith chūgham' arsan t-iascaire,
Solomon na mbreac,
'nuair dhúisínn oíche dhorcha
i lár na mara amuigh
's an d'rú ag seinm-tharrac ar
mo mhéir, mar seo, go sámh,
'sé deirinn le mo pháirtí istigh:
"sin é priocadh an deargáin!"'

Is nuair do sheinn an t-iascaire
an nóta ar a mhéir,
chonacamar á spreagadh aige
ceol fé leith an éisc.
Ach bhí deireadh seinnte ag Solomon
ar théid an deargáin —
mar nuair fhilleas-sa abhaile
ní théadh aon fhear i mbád.

(i)

Those relatives of mine who still survived,
the poet and the fisherman, sang out loud in unison:
'This is the fertile land where mothers have become extinct
and their daughters permanently exiled,
where sufficient pasture does not grow for donkeys
and people live on petty doles,
a land where no one now remembers a child at play,
or a boat being hoisted towards the sea,
or a dog, on leash to a whistled tune,
returning home from a long day's hunt.
This is the fertile land because we are assured –
from words we hear vibrating on the air –
that here reigns our white ancestral sea-gull
the talisman of our way of life;
so that it is we, the poet and the fisherman,
and some others of the chaste brethren with broken boots,
are the defenders of the life-pulse of our people.
And because of this we shall be praised by countless generations.
(And because of this a statue will most certainly be erected
to our memory in this our sea-gull sanctuary.)

(ii)

'Look here now' said the fisherman,
an aged Solomon,
'when I woke up at dark of night
in the ocean's maw
to find my finger tugging
on my fishing line like this,
I would say to my partner
"the bream is biting now".'

And when he replayed for us
the bream's special bite
we felt a kind of music
enveloping us all around.
But Solomon had ceased to play
on the rough ocean's strings –
when I returned home on a visit
no man took out his boat.

(iii)

'Tá cuireadh agaibh chun pósadh amárach'
— an file adúirt le flosc —
'beidh clagar ceoil ar siúl go maidin,
mar chleachtaí roimis seo.
Cuiríg díbh mar sin an alltacht
is bímís cruinn d'aonghuth:
'sé an fómhar céanna é, 's an t-earrach,
anso agus amuigh.

'Sé an fómhar céanna é, 's an t-earrach:
mar tar éis mórán dá dhua
ag cuardach iartaí an pharóiste, tá
dhá chreagar bheaga im chnuas.
Pósfad iad mé féin amárach
fé chreagar-cheangal cruaidh,
's beidh píopaireacht go háirithe
ar mo theallach-sa go buan.

'Sé an fómhar céanna é, 's an t-earrach:
á sea! ach féach mo dhabht:
ní haon eolaí ar chreagair mé
is ar a ngné táim dall;
's más fireannaigh mo pheidhre bheag
fágfar sinn gan chlann —
muna mbaineannóidh creatúr acu
le grásta Dé in am!'

(iv)

Ar mhair go fóill dem ghaolta, an file is an t-iascaire,
adúradar d'aon ghuth: 'Is neafaiseach
dar leat, a iomparaímíd crann ár bhfulanga
anso — ag biorú na deisbhéalaí 's ag seanchas!
Ach is fadó tá deireadh déanta le doilíos
sa dúthaigh seo; óir ní fulang fulang daoine
gan ribe beag den dóchas ann. 'S ní mó ár ndóchasna
go bhfillfeam ar ár ndúchas daonna arís
ná go dtabharfaidh an faoileán amuigh a haghaidh

(iii)

'You are expected at to-morrow's wedding',
the poet announced with zest,
'music clattering until morning
as in olden times:
forget then your astonishment
and let us all cry out:
'tis the same autumn, the same spring,
here as everywhere!

'Tis the same autumn, the same spring –
ah yes, for after dreadful trouble
combing the fireplaces in our parish
I've found a pair of crickets;
I'll marry them myself to-morrow,
tying them up in cricket-knots,
and there will be chirping a-plenty
on my hearth for evermore.'

'Tis the same autumn, the same spring?
– ah yes, but here's my doubt:
the ways of crickets are beyond me,
their sex a closed book,
and if both my crickets turn out male
we'll have no progeny,
unless one of them feminizes
(by the grace of God) in time.

(iv)

Those relatives of mine who still survived, the poet and the
fisherman,
sang out in unison: 'You find
we bear our cross of pain quite nonchalantly,
pointing up our repartee and gossiping.
We have dispensed with anguish,
for one suffers little where there is no shred of hope,
and the chance that we can still regain our human heritage
is no more than a wild seagull's dream

isteach fén tír. Bhí tráth is ghoill orainn go goirt
iad súd ba ghile linn a bheith ag leá os comhair
ár súl, 's ná feadramar go cruinn cé bhí ag cur
an chogaidh orainn. Táimíd imithe fé dheoigh,
áfach, laistíos, geall leis, de réim gach fulanga:
a bhfuil againn de dheora tá siad silte, a bhfuil
againn de mhianta tá siad múchta. Is go dearbh
duit, nuair shuímíd síos 'nár n-aonar tamall d'oíche
cois an luaithrigh, ní fhanann de mhíshuaimhneas
orainn tar éis ár léin dho-thuisceanta, ach go n-airímíd
go tiugh breoitiúil, ag brúchtadh aníos gan stad
mórdtimpeall orainn . . . bréantas corp nár cuireadh ins
an uaigh. 'S níl fear againn nach fearr leis bheith ag seanchaíocht
ná bheith á thórramh féin ar thinteán fuar'.

Eipealóg

Is dá bharr a fhilleas-sa, Baoithín, ar Oileán
Í, toisc gur duine mé mar chách; 's gurb é
is mó is cumas dom chun lot mo mhuintire
a leigheas, troscadh is urnaí. Is maith is léir
nach aon Chúchulainn mé a riastródh, 's a dhéanfadh
teasargan ar shlua 's na cúngracha, ach neach
atá oiriúnach ar oileán, ag ithe aráin
seagail tirim is piardóg bhruite, gorm glan
ón bhfarraige. Téim, mar sin, go humhal i measc
a bhfuil dem mhacasamhail-se fós ag guíochtaint ar
iargúl. . . . Is táim anois ag gairm go sollúnta
chūgham mo mháistir Colmcille. Agus gairmim
chūgham chomh maith 'na pháirt sin Pádraig agus Bríd
is Ciarán Chluana is fós naoimh Éireann uile, chun
go ndéanfaidís a n-iomrascáil gan trócaire
lem Thiarna — d'fhonn an ní nach dócha, an ní geall leis
dochreite, a theacht i gcrích go deimhnitheach.

Ach cé agaibhse anois a chreideann é —
an chaithréim geall leis dochreidte?

of making a home in the lush interior.
There was a time it caused us bitter hurt
that our loved ones were melting down before our eyes,
not knowing who was waging war against them;
we have long since gone beneath the limits of affliction –
what tears we had are shed, what desires we had
are quenched. And, quite honestly, when seated
by the ashes late at night, the main discomfort
we endure after all those years of incomprehensible
oppression, is that we sense continually oozing up
about us, the putrid smell of corpses left overground –
and there is no man among us who would not prefer to gossip
than keep vigil on his own body throughout the freezing night.

Epilogue

Being myself, Baoithín, the average man,
I fled back to Iona, knowing that
I best could help by fasting and by prayer
to cure the damage done my people.
I clearly am no Cúchulainn who, swelling up
in spasm, could free a multitude in deep distress –
rather one suited to small island life,
eating dry rye bread and boiled crayfish
fresh and pulsing from the sea.
So now I join with all of those who pray
in isolated places. And I summon
solemnly to my side my master Colmcille –
Patrick also, Brigid and Ciarán of Clonmacnoise,
indeed all the saints of Ireland –
to wrestle ruthlessly with Christ, my Lord,
so that the improbable, the nearly unbelievable,
will come to pass.

But which of you can still believe
the nearly unbelievable?

Nó cé chreidfeadh go n-éireodh an faoileán fiain
dá creig ar muir? 's go bhfeicfí í 'na héan mór bán
ag eitleánaíocht, oíche, trí's na spéartha soir,
ag múscailt gile ins gach áit 's ag leá na scáile
i súile dorcha — go dtúirlingeodh le liathadh
an lae ar loch intíre istigh, 's go lonnódh ann
'na hiontas croí, le saol na saol, ag oilithrigh.

Agus cé chreidfeadh fós go n-éireodh choíche arís
mo ghaolta tá ag dreo ar bhruach na huaighe? Nó go
n-athnuafadh anáil na beatha acu mo mhuintir uile
amuigh fén tír, tá titithe go fann i seirgluí?

Or who still believes that the wild Atlantic seagull
would one night vacate its ocean crag
and be seen a large white bird in flight
towards our eastern territories –
melting cataracts in darkened eyes,
rekindling brightness everywhere –
and landing finally at grey of dawn
on one of our interior lakes,
an everlasting wonder to hosts of pilgrims
who would visit there.

Or who can now believe that my closest relatives,
decaying and ready for the grave,
will rise again; or that their life-breath
will renew all my people who have fallen
into wasting sickness throughout the land.